Praise for *It's All Connected* . . .

Functions, and their representation by graphs, tables of values, and symbolic expressions, are among the most valuable tools of pure and applied mathematics. Based on extensive study of the challenges in learning about functions, *It's All Connected* is a valuable resource of easy-to-use activities that teachers in middle and high school mathematics will be able to apply in a variety of ways to develop and deepen key understandings and skills.

—James Fey, Professor Emeritus, University of Maryland

I am always searching for new and exciting ways to present algebraic concepts to my students—*It's All Connected* does just that. The resource offers a series of fifteen- to twenty-minute simple step-by-step lessons that easily can be incorporated into a larger curriculum or used on their own. The lessons make use of real-world applications that students will enjoy exploring, from the analysis of how rumors spread to the value of a motorcycle. *It's All Connected* also provides an excellent connection to the Common Core State Standards for modeling relationships through tables and graphs.

—Beth Klingher, math teacher, New Haven Public Schools, Connecticut

It's All Connected offers a fresh, unique approach to critical algebra concepts. With short, easy-to-use lessons, students can build conceptual understanding of graphs and related representations, beginning with intuitive descriptions and building toward equations. This could be particularly helpful for students who are visually oriented.

—Linda Dager Wilson, Director, Green Schools Project, Washington DC

Teachers committed to implementing the Common Core State Standards for Mathematical Practices will find *It's All Connected* of enormous value in understanding the role that context and relationships play in student learning. Van Dyke presents a collection of well-crafted, focused lessons with a unique approach to multiple representations for learning key ideas in algebra. Lessons are developed with an eye on both the learning progression and the mathematical horizon.

—M. Alejandra Sorto, Associate Professor, Department of Mathematics Texas State University, San Marcos, Texas

D1314114

It's All
Connected

The Power of
REPRESENTATION
to Build Algebraic Reasoning

Frances Van Dyke
SERIES EDITOR **CARMEN WHITMAN**

Math Solutions
150 Gate 5 Road
Sausalito, California, USA 94965
www.mathsolutions.com

Library of Congress Cataloging-in-Publication Data
CIP is on file with the Library of Congress.
ISBN 978-1-935099-42-0

Editor: Jamie Ann Cross
Production: Denise A. Botelho
Cover and interior design: Wanda Espana/Wee Design Group
Composition: Publishers' Design and Production Services, Inc.
Cover image: © Corbis

Printed in the United States of America on acid-free paper

16   15   14   13   12   AAP   1   2   3   4   5

A Message from Math Solutions

We at Math Solutions believe that teaching math well calls for increasing our understanding of the math we teach, seeking deeper insights into how students learn mathematics, and refining our lessons to best promote students' learning.

Math Solutions shares classroom-tested lessons and teaching expertise from our faculty of professional development consultants as well as from other respected math educators. Our publications are part of the nationwide effort we've made since 1984 that now includes

- more than five hundred face-to-face professional development programs each year for teachers and administrators in districts across the country;
- professional development books that span all math topics taught in kindergarten through high school;
- videos for teachers and for parents that show math lessons taught in actual classrooms;
- on-site visits to schools to help refine teaching strategies and assess student learning; and
- free online support, including grade-level lessons, book reviews, inservice information, and district feedback, all in our Math Solutions Online Newsletter.

For information about all of the products and services we have available, please visit our website at *www.mathsolutions.com.* You can also contact us to discuss math professional development needs by calling (800) 868-9092 or by sending an email to *info@mathsolutions.com.*

We're always eager for your feedback and interested in learning about your particular needs. We look forward to hearing from you.

To my husband Ted, my children Chris, Hugo, and Mary and to the memory of two other Hugos and two Nancys.

ACKNOWLEDGMENTS

I wish to thank the teachers that I have worked with and the editorial staff at Math Solutions.

Contents

Foreword by Carmen Whitman, Series Editor   *xi*

How to Use This Resource   *xiii*

Correlations to the Common Core State Standards   *xvii*

SECTION I   **Qualitative Graphs**

Overview   *2*

LESSON 1.1   **Prices in Washington**   *4*
Given a sentence, choose a graph

LESSON 1.2   **Value of a Portrait**   *8*
Given a graph, choose a sentence; draw graphs

LESSON 1.3   **Temperature for Tuesday**   *11*
Interpret and draw graphs; incorporate units of measurement

LESSON 1.4   **Population in Terms of Time**   *14*
Learn different ways to increase

LESSON 1.5   **Weather in Stony Creek, Rockville, and Boulder**   *19*
Learn different ways to decrease

LESSON 1.6   **Owning a Home**   *24*
Recognize and draw increasing functions with specified rates of change

LESSON 1.7   **Cars and Walking to School**   *27*
Recognize and draw decreasing functions with specified rates of change

LESSON 1.8   **Distance and Population**   *30*
Recognize and draw graphs with specified rates of change

LESSON 1.9   **An Antique, a Jewel, and a Car**   *33*
Compare and contrast values; create multiple graphs on one set of axes

LESSON 1.10   **Distance to a Bench**   *37*
Compare and contrast linear graphs

LESSON 1.11   **At the Beach**   *42*
Compare and contrast distance-versus-time graphs

Further Practice

FURTHER PRACTICE 1.A   **Value, Population, and Distance over Time**   *45*
Practice writing sentences describing graphs
(Can be done any time after Lesson 1.2)

FURTHER PRACTICE 1.B   **Your Choice and Animals at the Zoo**   *48*
Practice rates of change with increasing functions
(Can be done any time after Lesson 1.4)

FURTHER PRACTICE 1.C   **More Your Choice**   *50*
Practice with varying rates of change
(Can be done any time after Lesson 1.8)

SECTION II   Quantitative Graphs

Overview   *54*

LESSON 2.1   **Numbers on a Line**   *56*
Estimate points and tick marks along axes given certain values

LESSON 2.2   **Height of a Person**   *60*
Estimate scales along axes given height as a function of time

LESSON 2.3   **Value of a Car**   *65*
Read and interpret a quantitative graph of a decreasing function

LESSON 2.4   **Rising Real Estate Prices**   *68*
Interpret a quantitative graph of an increasing function with a decreasing rate of change

LESSON 2.5   **Perimeter of a Square**   *71*
Use the graph of the linear function $y = 4x$

LESSON 2.6   **Area of a Square**   *76*
Use the graph of the quadratic function $y = x^2$

LESSON 2.7   **A Rumor in the Classroom**   *81*
Interpret a graph with a point of inflection

LESSON 2.8   **Using a Motion Detector**   *85*
Interpret a quantitative graph of a decreasing function with a decreasing rate of change

LESSON 2.9   **Mark's Distance from the Cafeteria**   *90*
Work with a distance-versus-time graph

LESSON 2.10   **Value of a Boat**   *95*
Work with a decreasing function with an increasing rate of change

LESSON 2.11   **Rocket in the Air**   *100*
Work with a quadratic function that models the height of a rocket in terms of time

LESSON 2.12   **Beehive Rocket**   *103*
Draw the path of a rocket

SECTION III   Including Tables with Graphs

Overview   *108*

LESSON 3.1   **Spread of a Virus**   *110*
Lesson similar to Section II, table introduced at the end

LESSON 3.2   **Distance from a Dock**   *114*
Table and graph for a constant function

LESSON 3.3   **Distance from a Motion Detector**   *117*
Given a table, answer questions, and produce a graph

LESSON 3.4   **Value of an Antique**   *120*
Given a table, consider rate of change and graph

LESSON 3.5   **Value of a Motorcycle**   *124*
Given a linear relationship, produce a table and a graph

LESSON 3.6   **Distance from a House**   *129*
Given a graph, choose a table; given a table, choose a sentence

LESSON 3.7   **The Height of a Projectile**   *133*
*Given a quadratic function, answer questions. and produce
a table*

LESSON 3.8   **Throwing a Grapefruit!**   *137*
Further work with quadratic functions

FURTHER PRACTICE 3.A   **Your Choice**   *141*
Create your own example (Can be done any time after Lesson 3.5)

SECTION IV   Adding in Equations

Overview   *144*

LESSON 4.1   **Value of a Computer**   *146*
Work from description, to table, to graph, to equation

LESSON 4.2   **Purchase of a Jewel**   *150*
*Work from graph, to description, to table, to equation for an
increasing linear function*

LESSON 4.3   **Distance from a Building**   *153*
*Work from graph, to description, to table, to equation for a
decreasing linear function*

LESSON 4.4   **Stan Is Waiting**   *157*
Work with a constant function

LESSON 4.5   **Mary and the Pool**   *160*
Put it all together with an increasing linear function

LESSON 4.6   **The Cost of Pasta**   *163*
Work from description, to table, to graph, to equation for a cost function

LESSON 4.7   **Carl at the Gate**   *166*
Put it all together with a decreasing linear function

LESSON 4.8   **A Rocket in the Air**   *169*
Work from equation, to description, to graph, to table for a quadratic function

LESSON 4.9   **Another Rocket in the Air**   *174*
Understand quadratic functions

Index   **179**

Foreword

As a student of mathematics and even as a novice teacher, I often misunderstood algebraic reasoning. I thought it was all about symbolic manipulation, graphs, tables, and solving for a variable. Even though I was considered successful in mathematics and I made all As, I never made the connection among of these areas of mathematics. I thought everything was an isolated task. It wasn't until later in my teaching career that I began to see the connections between and among the different representations and how each representation told a story about the mathematics. Making the links among the representations brought new understanding to mathematics.

Sometimes the move from number operations to algebra (symbolic representation) is too drastic for students. They never learn to make connections between the two and therefore struggle with mathematics as they work through the middle grade years. Often students move to the abstract world of algebra without understanding what it is all about. Algebraic reasoning helps bridge the gap from numbers to symbolic rules and functions.

As students begin to use algebraic representations to understand mathematics and real-life problem situations, they begin to build their understanding of functions as they relate to life (everyday situations). Developing representational fluency sets the stage for success in their future learning of mathematics. *It's All Connected: The Power of Representation to Build Algebraic Reasoning* is an excellent resource to help students bridge the gap.

In this resource, Dr. Frances Van Dyke helps students develop algebraic reasoning and an understanding of the different representations for functions through a series of short lessons. These lessons often concentrate on one representation at a time. In doing so, teachers can easily isolate where students may be struggling as they move toward the symbolic world in mathematics. These lessons can be used to teach and assess students' knowledge as Dr. Van Dyke provides guidance and helpful hints for teachers as they teach the lessons. The Overview describes what each lesson entails, giving suggestions on prerequisite lessons and pointing out where students may be prone to misconceptions. The Teaching the Lesson section assists teachers in implement the lessons as it provides questions that teachers can ask in order to assess what students know.

It is refreshing to have a resource that helps teachers see and understand mathematics through different representations. After learning a concept, students are asked to demonstrate their understanding through additional problems and explain their thinking using appropriate mathematical language. These lessons provide a smooth progression through the world of representation. Students can focus on one aspect at a time, allowing them to use what they have learned to develop further understanding. These lessons make all aspects of algebraic reasoning accessible to both students and teachers and finally bring clarity to the abstract world of algebraic reasoning through representation, thus allowing our students to want to continue to learn mathematics.

It's All Connected: The Power of Representation to Build Algebraic Reasoning
will be beneficial to all teachers, from the novice to the experienced. This
resource provides a variety of ways that students can approach the mathematics and be successful. Answers to the lessons are provided, homework
assignments are suggested, and further practices are offered to push students'
thinking. This resource guides our students through the difficult world of representing mathematics in a variety of ways while making important connections along the way. Using this resource, we can help our students develop a
firm grasp on understanding different representations. With this understanding, students will be able to comprehend the use of properties of operations
as they develop their mathematics from arithmetic to algebra, keeping them
interested in learning and being successful with mathematics.

Carmen Whitman
Series Editor
Director of Mathematics for All Consulting

How to Use This Resource

Overview

It's All Connected was created in the belief that concentrating on graphs can be a highly effective approach to mastering algebraic concepts. The 40 lessons, which include reproducible student pages, ease students and teachers into algebra through the study of the graphical representation of functions. Each lesson seamlessly supports core curriculum.

The short lessons in this resource (each takes approximately fifteen to twenty-five minutes) are ideal for implementation with students in the classroom, and they can also be used by teachers for the purpose of professional development. For classroom use, these mini-lessons should be taught one to three times a week throughout the academic year.

Why This Resource?

Research reveals that many students struggle with or never develop the ability to easily move from one representation for a function to another. Because this is a necessary skill for mathematical understanding, these students are at risk for failure in mathematics. Research also reveals that prospective teachers have especially low scores on assessments that evaluate flexibility between visual and algebraic representations and flexibility with real-life situations. This resource provides the support needed to significantly improve both students' and teachers' algebraic understanding.

Learning beginning algebra is much enhanced by the early introduction of graphs and indeed can be first approached using graphs. There is a natural progression from qualitative graphs (graphs without scale), to quantitative graphs (graphs with scale), to tables, and finally to equations. By describing relationships between familiar real-world quantities, the graphs in this resource support students (and teachers) in perceiving algebra as practical and concrete from the start.

> "Studies show that flexibility with visual representations is the most important factor in predicting [teachers'] content knowledge. This suggests that it would be beneficial for teacher educators to provide prospective elementary and middle school teachers more opportunities to solve problems with graphical representations of linear functions."
>
> —*Journal of Mathematics Education, June 2010*

WHAT IS THE PHILOSOPHY OF THIS RESOURCE?

Over the years, mathematics teachers have been urged to make profound changes in content, teaching style, and assessment. The traditional approach of presenting a rule, giving a few examples, and then working a series of exercises based on the examples is not seen as the optimal method of promoting true learning. The current philosophy is that the emphasis should be on student thinking, problem solving, and comprehension of underlying concepts. Moreover, applications should play a prominent role. Students need to be given opportunities to formulate problems, reason mathematically, make connections between mathematical ideas, and write about mathematics. The focus is away from symbolic manipulation and courses that concentrate on developing a set of procedural skills.

This resource naturally aligns itself with the current philosophy in mathematics education. Understanding the graphical representations of functions cannot be achieved in a procedural fashion. Applications are involved in every lesson, and students are consistently asked to formulate their own problems. Interpreting graphs requires students to think on an abstract level.

Changing outlook, content, and teaching style is not an easy process. It tests and taxes the creativity, commitment, time, adaptability, and energy of teachers, departments, and administrators alike. A related challenge is the prevalence of high-stakes testing and the pressure teachers feel to "teach to the test." The combination of change and pressure is particularly hard on middle school teachers who often have to teach more than one subject area and are not required to be certified in mathematics. It is the goal of this work to make the graphical representation of functions not only accessible to students and teachers but also an exciting new domain that they will want to explore and incorporate fully into their base of mathematical knowledge.

> "It is the goal of this work to make the graphical representation of functions not only accessible to students and teachers but also an exciting new domain that they will want to explore and incorporate fully into their base of mathematical knowledge."

Thinking Abstractly

In each of the forty mini-lessons, the initial effort to picture a relationship prompts students to think on an abstract level. This is an excellent way for students to understand the concept of a function—seeing how one quantity relates to another. Students first recognize the appropriate graph to use and then move on to creating their own examples. This approach allows students to perform the abstract process of representation and analysis with graphs before having to deal with algebraic notation. Producing their own graphs naturally assimilates students to the mathematics standards of communication and representation.

Analyzing Change

Analyzing change is another major component of this work. The lessons begin by examining change that is constant and then introduce the notion that change can be represented as occurring increasingly faster or slower. This is a key concept in calculus and should be introduced in middle school by looking at and interpreting the shapes of curves. Both researchers and teachers have noted that students often fail to see that variables vary. Students tend to see x as some specific (albeit perhaps unknown) quantity. A graph emphasizes the fact that x varies, taking on different values with movement along the horizontal axis.

Moving from Graphs to Equations

Throughout the middle school and high school mathematics curricula, students struggle with the concept of underlying equivalence. Changes in form and representation often cause students to lose sight of the fact that they are producing something equivalent to what they started with. This is particularly true when students move from an equation to a graph. Because a graph and an equation look so different, students do not grasp the fact that they are two representations of the same set of points. In the research literature, this problem is referred to as "not seeing the Cartesian connection." The use of a graphics calculator can make graphs far more accessible but does not necessarily help students see the Cartesian connection. The fact that every point on the graph satisfies the equation and that every solution to the equation is a point on the graph often comes as a surprise to students and takes them a long time to assimilate.

Teachers are urged to emphasize and reiterate often the fundamental relationship between graphs and equations.

The Importance of the Graphical Representation of Functions

Before the advent of graphics calculators, graphs played a much smaller role in the high school mathematics curriculum. Graphs were, for the most part, imperfectly produced by students, and the exercise to make a graph was the end, in and of itself. With the introduction of calculators that produce graphs, the graphical representation of a function can be as useful as and sometimes more useful than the equation corresponding to the function. The graph provides an overall picture of the relationship and indicates intervals of change.

The increase in attention to the graphical representation of functions makes it important for students to come into high school comfortable using graphs and able to understand the fundamental principles associated with them. Because this emphasis is relatively new, not a great deal of material about it is available for use by middle school teachers. This resource book provides that material. By using it in the classroom, teachers can help students thoroughly understand the fundamental principles of graphs and the underlying connections between graphs and equations.

How Is This Resource Organized?

It's All Connected has been carefully developed and organized to make it helpful for and easy to use by teachers. Familiarity with the graphical representation of functions is not assumed.

As outlined in the Contents, this resource has forty minilessons presented in four sections:

- Section I: eleven (11) lessons on qualitative graphs (picturing relationships students are familiar with)
- Section II: twelve (12) lessons on quantitative graphs (emphasizing units of measurement)
- Section III: eight (8) lessons on using tables with graphs
- Section IV: nine (9) lessons on equations (naturally arising from the data and graphs)

There are more lessons on graphs than on tables/equations because graphs are the subject proven to be most unfamiliar to teachers.

Each lesson takes between fifteen and twenty-five minutes to complete and contains two main parts: Teaching Suggestions and a Reproducible. The Teaching Suggestions section is divided into the following subsections:

Calculators as "Transformer" Toys

I worked with a ninth-grade teacher several years ago, when so-called Transformer toys were popular. With these toys, one could start with a robot and, through a few specific twists, produce a boat or some other totally unrelated object. It occurred to the teacher and me that students were looking at calculators like Transformer toys: One fed in an equation and out came a graph, but there was no real relationship between the two.

OVERVIEW

The overview summarizes the content of the lesson. It specifies the concepts to be introduced or reviewed and indicates the tasks that students will be required to perform.

CLASS TIME

Duration of lesson is noted; the times vary between 15 and 25 minutes.

PREREQUISITES

The prerequisites list previous lessons that should have been covered before attempting the current one, as well as concepts it is assumed students have mastered.

TEACHING THE LESSON

This section makes suggestions as to how to go about teaching the lesson and often gives specific questions that can be asked. It discusses possible misconceptions and highlights concepts students traditionally have trouble understanding.

HOMEWORK AND ASSESSMENT

In Lesson 1.3, a suggestion is made as to how to assess the problems given for homework in the book. In general, two homework problems are provided for each lesson. These are optional and reinforce the ideas in the lesson.

ANSWERS (FOR BOTH THE STUDENT RECORDING SHEET AND HOMEWORK)

In-depth answers are provided for all questions asked.

EXTEND THE LEARNING

Extra problems are given for students who are looking for more of a challenge. Answers are provided.

DO I NEED TO DO THE LESSONS IN ORDER?

You should follow the order of the four sections, but you may decide not to do every lesson in every section. Once the class has achieved a comfort level with qualitative graphs (Section I), it can move on to quantitative graphs (Section II). The point at which this occurs may vary from class to class, so you may not need to go through every lesson in Section I if you feel your class has a firm grasp of the ideas. Likewise, you may move on to tables (Section III) and then equations (Section IV) without completing every lesson in the sections that precede them. Exercises in later sections that refer back to earlier lessons are clearly marked. On occasion, students seem to understand a concept but then lose sight of it later, when ensuing material is covered. If this should happen, you can easily go back to review a concept without disrupting the flow of the material.

The goal of this work is to give students a solid foundation in the graphical representation of functions which will help them throughout high school and college.

Correlations to the Common Core State Standards

In this correlation you will find some lessons that span several grade levels. A lesson can be used as an introduction to different types of representations, developing the student's understanding of the general nature of graphs, tables, or equations. It can be used later in the student's career to refresh their understanding or to assess their knowledge of a topic as they proceed with the development of more complex problems. Lessons, homework suggestions, and extensions that encompass the lessons were all considered when creating the correlation.

Modeling is best interpreted not as a collection of isolated topics but in relation to other standards. Making mathematical models is a Standard for Mathematical Practice, and specific modeling standards appear throughout the high school standards indicated by a star symbol (★). The star symbol sometimes appears on the heading for a group of standards; in that case, it should be understood to apply to all standards in that group (corestandards.org/assets/CCSSI_Math Standards.pdf).

Grade 6

Domain: Ratios and Proportional Relationships—6.RP

Understand ratio concepts and use ratio reasoning to solve problems.

3. Use ratio and rate reasoning to solve real-world and mathematical problems (e.g., by reasoning about tables of equivalent ratios, tape diagrams, double number line diagrams, or equations).	
a. Make tables of equivalent ratios relating quantities with whole-number measurements, find missing values in the tables, and plot the pairs of values on the coordinate plane. Use tables to compare ratios.	Lessons 3.5 and 4.6
b. Solve unit rate problems including those involving unit pricing and constant speed. *For example, if it took 7 hours to mow 4 lawns, then at that rate, how many lawns could be mowed in 35 hours? At what rate were lawns being mowed?*	Lessons 1.1, 1.4, 1.5, 1.7, 2.4, 2.5, and 3.5

The Number System — 6.NS

Apply and extend previous understandings of numbers to the system of rational numbers.

6. Understand a rational number as a point on the number line. Extend number line diagrams and coordinate axes familiar from previous grades to represent points on the line and in the plane with negative number coordinates.	
b. Understand signs of numbers in ordered pairs as indicating locations in quadrants of the coordinate plane; recognize that when two ordered pairs differ only by signs, the locations of the points are related by reflections across one or both axes.	Lesson 2.1
c. Find and position integers and other rational numbers on a horizontal or vertical number line diagram; find and position pairs of integers and other rational numbers on a coordinate plane.	Lesson 2.1
8. Solve real-world and mathematical problems by graphing points in all four quadrants of the coordinate plane. Include use of coordinates and absolute value to find distances between points with the same first coordinate or the same second coordinate.	Lesson 2.1

Expressions and Equations — 6.EE

Reason about and solve one-variable equations and inequalities.

5. Understand solving an equation or inequality as a process of answering a question: which values from a specified set, if any, make the equation or inequality true? Use substitution to determine whether a given number in a specified set makes an equation or inequality true.	Lessons 4.1, 4.2, 4.5, and 4.6

Grade 6

6.	Use variables to represent numbers and write expressions when solving a real-world or mathematical problem; understand that a variable can represent an unknown number, or, depending on the purpose at hand, any number in a specified set.	Lessons 4.1 and 4.5
7.	Solve real-world and mathematical problems by writing and solving equations of the form $x + p = q$ and $px = q$ for cases in which p, q and x are all nonnegative rational numbers.	Lessons 4.4 and 4.5
Represent and analyze quantitative relationships between dependent and independent variables.		
9.	Use variables to represent two quantities in a real-world problem that change in relationship to one another; write an equation to express one quantity, thought of as the dependent variable, in terms of the other quantity, thought of as the independent variable. Analyze the relationship between the dependent and independent variables using graphs and tables, and relate these to the equation. *For example, in a problem involving motion at constant speed, list and graph ordered pairs of distances and times, and write the equation $d = 65t$ to represent the relationship between distance and time.*	Lessons 1.1, 1.2, 1.3, 1.4, 1.A, 4.2, 4.3, 4.5, and 4.6

Grade 7

Ratios and Proportional Relationships — 7.RP

Analyze proportional relationships and use them to solve real-world and mathematical problems.		
2.	Recognize and represent proportional relationships between quantities.	
	a. Decide whether two quantities are in a proportional relationship (e.g., by testing for equivalent ratios in a table or graphing on a coordinate plane and observing whether the graph is a straight line through the origin).	Lessons 1.7, 1.8, 1.9, 1.10, 2.5, and 4.6
	b. Identify the constant of proportionality (unit rate) in tables, graphs, equations, diagrams, and verbal descriptions of proportional relationships.	Lessons 1.7, 1.8, 1.9, 1.10, 4.6, and 4.7
	c. Represent proportional relationships by equations. *For example, if total cost t is proportional to the number n of items purchased at a constant price p, the relationship between the total cost and the number of items can be expressed as* t = pn.	Lessons 1.8, 1.9, 1.10, and 4.6
	d. Explain what a point (x,y) on the graph of a proportional relationship means in terms of the situation, with special attention to the points (0,0) and (1,r) where r is the unit rate.	Lessons 2.5, 3.6, 3.A, and 4.6

Expressions and Equations — 7.EE

Solve real-life and mathematical problems using numerical and algebraic expressions and equations.		
4.	Use variables to represent quantities in a real-world or mathematical problem, and construct simple equations and inequalities to solve problems by reasoning about the quantities.	
	a. Solve word problems leading to equations of the form $px + q = r$ and $p(x + q) = r$, where p, q, and r are specific rational numbers. Solve equations of these forms fluently. Compare an algebraic solution to an arithmetic solution, identifying the sequence of the operations used in each approach. *For example, the perimeter of a rectangle is 54 cm. Its length is 6 cm. What is its width?*	Lessons 4.4, and 4.6, and 4.7

Grade 8

Expressions and Equations — 8.EE

Understand the connections between proportional relationships, lines, and linear equations.

5.	Graph proportional relationships, interpreting the unit rate as the slope of the graph. Compare two different proportional relationships represented in different ways. *For example, compare a distance-time graph to a distance-time equation to determine which of two moving objects has greater speed.*	Lessons 1.10, 1.11, 3.5, and 4.6
8.	Analyze and solve pairs of simultaneous linear equations.	
	a. Understand that solutions to a system of two linear equations in two variables correspond to points of intersection of their graphs, because points of intersection satisfy both equations simultaneously.	Lessons 1.10 and 1.11
	c. Solve real-world and mathematical problems leading to two linear equations in two variables. *For example, given coordinates for two pairs of points, determine whether the line through the first pair of points intersects the line through the second pair.*	Lessons 2.8 and 2.9

Functions — 8.F

Define, evaluate, and compare functions.

1.	Understand that a function is a rule that assigns to each input exactly one output. The graph of a function is the set of ordered pairs consisting of an input and the corresponding output.[1]	All Lessons
Note: Function notation is not required in Grade 8.		
2.	Compare properties of two functions each represented in a different way (algebraically, graphically, numerically in tables, or by verbal descriptions). *For example, given a linear function represented by a table of values and a linear function represented by an algebraic expression, determine which function has the greater rate of change.*	Lessons 3.1 and 3.6
3.	Interpret the equation $y = mx + b$ as defining a linear function, whose graph is a straight line; give examples of functions that are not linear. *For example, the function $A = s^2$ giving the area of a square as a function of its side length is not linear because its graph contains the points (1,1), (2,4) and (3,9), which are not on a straight line.*	Lessons 1.B, 2.4, 2.6, 4.5, 4.7, 4.8, and 4.9
4.	Construct a function to model a linear relationship between two quantities. Determine the rate of change and initial value of the function from a description of a relationship or from two (x,y) values, including reading these from a table or from a graph. Interpret the rate of change and initial value of a linear function in terms of the situation it models, and in terms of its graph or a table of values.	Lessons 1.1, 1.2, 1.3, 1.C, 2.3, 2.7, 3.2, 4.3, 4.4, 4.5, and 4.7
5.	Describe qualitatively the functional relationship between two quantities by analyzing a graph (e.g., where the function is increasing or decreasing, linear or nonlinear). Sketch a graph that exhibits the qualitative features of a function that has been described verbally.	Lessons 1.3, 1.4, 1.5, 1.6, 1.7, 1.8, 1.9, 1.10, 1.B, 2.3, 2.8, 2.9, 3.6, 4.3, 4.4, 4.5, 4.7, 4.8, and 4.9

Algebra

Creating Equations — A-CED

Create equations that describe numbers or relationships.

1. Create equations and inequalities in one variable and use them to solve problems. *Include equations arising from linear and quadratic functions, and simple rational and exponential functions.*	Lessons 4.2, 4.6, 4.7, 4.8, and 4.9
2. Create equations in two or more variables to represent relationships between quantities; graph equations on coordinate axes with labels and scales.	Lessons: 2.9, 4.5, 4.6, 4.7, 4.8, and 4.9

Reasoning with Equations and Inequalities — A-REI

Solve equations and inequalities in one variable.

3. Solve linear equations and inequalities in one variable, including equations with coefficients represented by letters.	Lessons 4.2 and 4.4

Represent and solve equations and inequalities graphically.

10. Understand that the graph of an equation in two variables is the set of all its solutions plotted in the coordinate plane, often forming a curve (which could be a line).	Lessons 2.3, 2.4, 2.5, 2.6, 2.7, 2.8, 3.3, 3.4, 3.7, 4.8, and 4.9

Functions

Interpreting Functions — F-IF

Understand the concept of a function and use function notation.

1. Understand that a function from one set (called the *domain*) to another set (called the *range*) assigns to each element of the domain exactly one element of the range. If f is a function and x is an element of its domain, then $f(x)$ denotes the output of f corresponding to the input x. The graph of f is the graph of the equation $y = f(x)$.	All Lessons

Interpret functions that arise in applications in terms of the context.

4. For a function that models a relationship between two quantities, interpret key features of graphs and tables in terms of the quantities, and sketch graphs showing key features given a verbal description of the relationship. *Key features include: intercepts; intervals where the function is increasing, decreasing, positive, or negative; relative maximums and minimums; symmetries; end behavior; and periodicity.* ★	Lessons 1.3, 1.4, 1.5, 1.6, 1.7, 1.10, 2.2, 2.4, 3.8, 4.5, 4.8, and 4.9

Analyze functions using different representations.

7. Graph functions expressed symbolically and show key features of the graph, by hand in simple cases and using technology for more complicated cases. ★	
a. Graph linear and quadratic functions and show intercepts, maxima, and minima.	Lessons 2.9, 2.11, 2.12, 3.7, 4.5, 4.8 and 4.9

Building Functions — F-BF

Build a function that models a relationship between two quantities

1. Write a function that describes a relationship between two quantities. ★	
b. Combine standard function types using arithmetic operations. *For example, build a function that models the temperature of a cooling body by adding a constant function to a decaying exponential, and relate these functions to the model.*	Lessons 1.3, 1.5, and 2.10

Functions	
Linear, Quadratic, and Exponential Models ★— F-LE	
Construct and compare linear, quadratic, and exponential models and solve problems	
1. Distinguish between situations that can be modeled with linear functions and with exponential functions.	
b. Recognize situations in which one quantity changes at a constant rate per unit interval relative to another.	Lessons 2.5, 2.7, 4.5, and 4.6

It's All
Connected

Qualitative Graphs

Overview

The lessons in this section, each intended to take 15 to 25 minutes to complete, introduce the idea of using a graph to represent a relationship between two quantities. The graphical model is a powerful tool when used to depict a relationship and can be accessed without algebraic symbolism. It is thus possible for students to do these lessons before being introduced to variables or as a welcome relief when struggling to find appropriate algebraic representations for functions.

The lessons focus on the fundamental idea of the graphical representation of a function and teach students to read graphs from a global perspective. The lessons introduce the notion of increasing and decreasing functions and move on to increasing and decreasing rates of change. Initially, a descriptive sentence is given and students must choose an appropriate graph. Next, a graph is given and students must choose an appropriate descriptive sentence. Students are then asked to draw their own graphs for specified sentences and to write their own sentences for given graphs.

The notion of increasing and decreasing rates of change is often hard for students to grasp and remember, so it is the focus of Lessons 1.4–1.8.

Further Practice exercises are provided if further work is needed on the topic. Units of measurement are introduced, although no scale is given until Section II.

A HISTORY NOTE

Using a graph to represent the relationship between two quantities is a relatively new invention, developed between 1750 and 1800. A Scottish engineer and political economist, William Playfair (1759–1823), is credited with first using graphs to display statistical data.

CONNECTING TO THE COMMON CORE

Representing and interpreting data is a fundamental category in the Common Core State Standards for first grade through high school. For more on the Common Core connections, see page xvii, Correlations to the Common Core State Standards.

Lessons

LESSON 1.1   **Prices in Washington**   *4*
Given a sentence, choose a graph.

LESSON 1.2   **Value of a Portrait**   *8*
Given a graph, choose a sentence; draw graphs.

LESSON 1.3   **Temperature for Tuesday**   *11*
Interpret and draw graphs; incorporate units of measurement.

LESSON 1.4   **Population in Terms of Time**   *14*
Learn different ways to increase.

LESSON 1.5   **Weather in Stony Creek, Rockville, and Boulder**   *19*
Learn different ways to decrease.

LESSON 1.6   **Owning a Home**   *24*
Recognize and draw increasing functions with specified rates of change.

LESSON 1.7   **Cars and Walking to School**   *27*
Recognize and draw decreasing functions with specified rates of change.

LESSON 1.8   **Distance and Population**   *30*
Recognize and draw graphs with specified rates of change.

LESSON 1.9   **An Antique, a Jewel, and a Car**   *33*
Compare and contrast values; create multiple graphs on one set of axes.

LESSON 1.10   **Distance to a Bench**   *37*
Compare and contrast linear graphs.

LESSON 1.11   **At the Beach**   *42*
Compare and contrast distance-versus-time graphs.

FURTHER PRACTICE 1.A   **Value, Population, and Distance over Time**   *45*
Practice writing sentences describing graphs. (Can be done after Lesson 1.2)

FURTHER PRACTICE 1.B   **Your Choice and Animals at the Zoo**   *48*
Practice rates of change with increasing functions. (Can be done after Lesson 1.5)

FURTHER PRACTICE 1.C   **Make Your Own Example**   *50*
Practice with varying rates of change. (Can be done after Lesson 1.8)

Prices in Washington

Given a sentence, choose a graph.

Overview

> **Class Time:** 15 minutes
>
> **Prerequisites:** Some exposure to the Cartesian (*xy*) plane is preferable, although not necessary.

This lesson introduces students to the idea that a relationship between two quantities can be represented using a graph. Students will learn how to read a graph in its entirety. They will also start to gain an appreciation of how to recognize a decreasing function versus an increasing function.

Teaching the Lesson

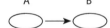

MATH MATTERS

Function

A *function* is a correspondence between a set A and set B, where each element in A is assigned to one and only one element in B, like this:

A   B

Each graph on Student Recording Sheet 1.1 shows the relationship between two quantities: price and time. In every case, the relationship is a *function*, meaning that for each moment in time, there is only one price.

Many of the applications encountered in mathematics involve the change of some quantity in terms of time. Students will thus frequently find the label *Time* along the *x*-axis (horizontal axis).

The axes of the *xy* plane are provided for the purpose of orientation. Students tend to identify the axes with the relationship, so the function is meaningless unless the axes are present. This can be problematic for students when they take statistics or calculus.

To reinforce the fact that the relationship is distinct from the axes, the function is formatted as a thicker line on each graph. Point this out, identifying the *x*-axis (horizontal axis) as the line on which increasing units of time will be marked and the *y*-axis (vertical axis) as the line on which value in dollars will be marked.

Exercises about value or price in terms of time are good to start out with and to come back to if students are having trouble with a concept. These exercises will be familiar to some students and easy for others to pick up.

Remind students that we read graphs from left to right, as the tendency is to look at graphs only as pictures. As we move to the right, time is passing. Scanning the graph from left to right, we see how value or price changes as time passes. We move our eyes along the horizontal axis and while doing so decide whether the curve is rising, falling, or staying the same. This will indicate whether the value or price is increasing, decreasing, or remaining constant.

Students in high school often fail to consider the overall trend when looking at a graph. They focus on points as they are so often just asked about points and not what the overall picture tells them. Those who do look at the overall trend may have problems trying to relate what the graph looks like to the situation. Say a graph depicts speed versus time of a person walking and it looks like a hill. You could ask, "Do you think the person is going up a hill and then down a hill or first going downhill and then uphill? Justify your answer." If the student sees the graph as a picture of a hill, he might answer the person is first going uphill and then downhill. If the student reads the graph, she sees that speed increases and then decreases so it is more likely the person is first going downhill and then uphill.

In this lesson, because there are no units on the graphs, students are forced to look at each graph in its entirety. This is a habit that students should maintain when they are creating graphs with specified qualities.

For the most part, we will be looking at the first quadrant of the xy plane, in which both quantities are positive. You can point out that only one-quarter of the plane is being represented. The axes cross one another, rather than meet at the corner, to subtly suggest the existence of the other three quadrants.

Homework and Assessment

After students complete their recording sheet, ask them to write an appropriate sentence describing the graph featured in 2c on the Student Recording Sheet—for example, *The price of the condo first fell but then rose*. Choose one of the other graphs, and ask students to come up with an appropriate sentence different from any on the Student Recording Sheet. (An appropriate sentence will relate value to time correctly, but the object being valued can be of the student's choosing.) Encourage students to look over their Student Recording Sheets carefully and make sure they understand all of the answers.

Answers to Lesson 1.1 Student Recording Sheet and Homework

STUDENT RECORDING SHEET

1. b; As time passes, the price rises. Be sure students associate time passing with moving their eyes from left to right.
2. d; Point out that a horizontal line indicates that the value does not change as time passes. As we move our eyes from left to right, the value remains the same.
3. b; As time passes, the price goes up and then goes down.
4. a; As time passes, the price falls.

HOMEWORK

For the homework, the sentences justifying the answers should include the phrase "As time passes." Students have a tendency just to respond "It rises" or "It falls."

> **Extend the Learning:** Explain to a friend how to picture the relationship between value and time using a graph.

Student _____ Class _____ Date _____

For each problem, choose the graph that best matches the situation described. Also write a sentence explaining why you chose the graph you did.

1. The price of a house in Washington is going up.

a.

b.

c.

d.

_____

_____

2. The price of riding the Metro is staying the same.

a.

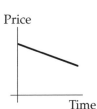

b.

c.

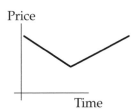

d.

_____

_____

From *It's All Connected: The Power of Representation to Build Algebraic Reasoning, Grades 6–9* by Frances Van Dyke. © 2012 by Scholastic Inc. Permission granted to photocopy for nonprofit use in a classroom or similar place dedicated to face-to-face educational purposes. Downloadable at www.mathsolutions.com/itsallconnectedalgebrareproducibles.

3. The price of gas first increased and then decreased.

a.

b.

c.

d.

_____

_____

4. The price of fruit is coming down.

a.

b.

c.

d.

_____

_____

Value of a Portrait

Given a graph, choose a sentence; draw graphs.

Overview

Class Time: 25 minutes

Prerequisites: Do Lesson 1.1. Familiarity with the process of reading a simple sentence and then choosing the corresponding graph will make interpreting a graph easier.

In Lesson 1.1, students chose the graph that best matched each sentence given. In the first part of the lesson, students choose the sentence that best corresponds to the graph. In the second part of the lesson, students are asked to draw graphs that correspond to sentences. The graphs are slightly more complex than those from Lesson 1.1. Again, students should look at the graph from a global point of view.

Teaching the Lesson

The first task on the Lesson 1.2 Student Recording Sheet should be done by the whole class. Discuss how to recognize whether a function is increasing or decreasing at a certain point. Get students to explain that in reading a graph, we start at the left. As we move to the right in reading this graph, the value falls, then remains constant for a time, and then increases.

The second task on the Student Recording Sheet can be done by students in groups of two or three. Working in groups, have students draw a graph for each remaining sentence. Encourage students to draw the graph of the relationship in a different color from the color used for the axes. Remind students once more that we read graphs from left to right and that the axes are present for the purpose of orientation.

For each graph, have two students from different groups come to the board and draw their groups' answers. If students forget to label the axes, remind them to do so. Ask the other students in the class to compare the two answers. Both answers may be correct but subtly different. For instance, one may have the value increasing or remaining constant longer than the other.

Pick one of the graphs, and ask the following key questions. (**Note:** Students will be asked to write down the answers to these questions in subsequent lessons.)

? KEY QUESTIONS

1. This graph shows a relationship between which two quantities? (Value and time)

2. What are some of the different ways we measure time? (In seconds, minutes, hours, days, months, years, decades, centuries)

3. For this graph, what would you guess are the units of measurement for time? (Years)
4. How do we measure value? (Dollars or some other currency. Tell students that we say, "The units of measurement along the horizontal axis are years, and the units of measurement along the vertical axis are dollars.")

Students often think that in math classes, there is only one correct answer to a problem. The first homework problem illustrates that this is not true when drawing qualitative graphs.

Homework and Assessment

For homework after finishing the Student Recording Sheet, ask students to do one of the following exercises:

1. Suppose a teacher asks 25 students to draw graphs corresponding to this statement: *The price of cotton first increased and then decreased.* Is it possible for the students to submit 25 different answers, all of which are correct? Explain your answer.
2. We have used time as one of the quantities in each graph. This does not always have to be the case. Try to draw a graph corresponding to the following sentence, with *Width* along the *x*-axis and *Length* along the *y*-axis: *As the width of the rectangle increased, the length remained the same.*

Answers to Lesson 1.2 Student Recording Sheet and Homework

STUDENT RECORDING SHEET

1. Sentence b

2. Sentence a:

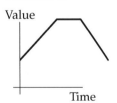

3. Sentence c:

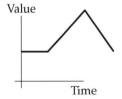

4. Sentence d:

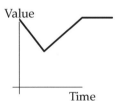

HOMEWORK

1. Yes, it is possible for students to submit 25 different answers, all of which are correct. There is an infinite number of correct answers.
2. The graph should present a horizontal line. Problems involving horizontal lines sometimes give students trouble. They often want to put a single point when graphing a quantity that stays the same, and later, when they see an equation of the form $y = 5$, they are uncertain what to do.

Extend the Learning: You have now had to draw a graph given a sentence and write a sentence given a graph. Which is easier and why?

Student _____ Class _____ Date _____

1. Consider the following graph. Which of the following sentences (a–d) best matches the graph? Explain your reasoning.

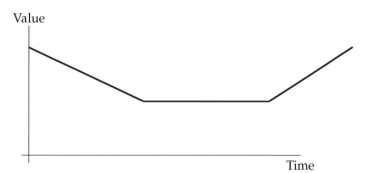

   a. The value of the portrait increased for awhile, then held constant, and then decreased.

   b. The value of the portrait decreased for awhile, then remained the same, and then increased.

   c. The value of the portrait remained the same for awhile, then increased, and then decreased.

   d. The value of the portrait decreased, then increased, and then held constant.

2. For each sentence you did not choose, draw a graph to match it. Be sure to label the axes.

From *It's All Connected: The Power of Representation to Build Algebraic Reasoning, Grades 6–9* by Frances Van Dyke. © 2012 by Scholastic Inc.
Permission granted to photocopy for nonprofit use in a classroom or similar place dedicated to face-to-face educational purposes.
Downloadable at www.mathsolutions.com/itsallconnectedalgebrareproducibles.

Temperature for Tuesday

Interpret and draw graphs; incorporate units of measurement.

Overview

Class Time: 25 minutes

Prerequisites: Students should have some experience with interpreting graphs and drawing graphs (see Lessons 1.1 and 1.2).

In this lesson, students put together the skills learned in Lessons 1.1 and 1.2. Here, they must both interpret and draw graphs. Units of measurement are also introduced in this lesson. (**Note:** Science teachers sometimes express concern that units of measurement are not emphasized enough in math classes. This lesson will help alleviate that concern.)

Teaching the Lesson

Do the first problem on the Lesson 1.3 Student Recording Sheet as a whole class, and then have students do the remaining two problems in small groups. Refer back to the "Teaching the Lesson" sections in Lessons 1.1 and 1.2 for support in addressing any misconceptions.

Homework and Assessment

For homework after finishing the Student Recording Sheet, assign the following problem. Consider assessing students' answers on a scale of 1–3, as shown here.

Assessment Scale

3 Solid answer with good detail

2 Some part of answer incorrect but basic idea understood

1 Some effort made but basic idea not understood

Draw a graph corresponding to this sentence: *As the weight of the food substance increased, the price paid for it also increased.*

a. What is the quantity along the *x*-axis? What are the units of measurement?

b. What is the quantity along the *y*-axis? What are the units of measurement?

STUDENT RECORDING SHEET

1.
   a. The graph shows the relationship between temperature and time.
   b. Possible sentence: *After midnight, the temperature dropped, then rose during the day, and then fell once more as dawn came on.*
   c. The units of measurement are hours.
   d. The units of measurement are degrees.

2.
   a. The graph shows the relationship between distance and time.
   b. Possible sentence: *She walked toward the building and then stopped to talk to a friend.*
   c. The units of measurement are seconds.
   d. The units of measurement are feet.

3. Value

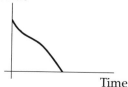

Time

The value of the book decreased the longer it was used.

HOMEWORK

   a. The quantity along the *x*-axis is weight of food. The units of measurement are pounds or ounces (for U.S. system of weight).
   b. The quantity along the *y*-axis is price. The units of measurement are dollars or cents (for U.S. currency).

> **Extend the Learning:** Sometimes, things increase at a faster and faster rate, and other times, they increase but more and more slowly. How can this be shown on a graph? (For the answer, see the "Extend the Lesson" section in Lesson 1.4.)

Student _____ Class _____ Date _____

Answer all questions for each of the following.

1. Here is a graph for Tuesday's temperatures.

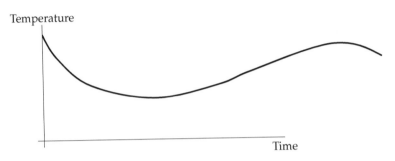

a. This graph shows a relationship between which two quantities?

b. Write a sentence that describes the graph.

c. What are the units of measurement along the horizontal axis?

d. What are the units of measurement along the vertical axis?

2. Distance

a. This graph shows a relationship between which two quantities?

b. Write a sentence that describes the graph.

c. What are the units of measurement along the horizontal axis?

d. What are the units of measurement along the vertical axis?

3. Draw a graph that represents the value of your textbook as time passes from the first day of school. Write a few sentences explaining your graph.

LESSON 1.4 Population in Terms of Time

Learn different ways to increase.

Overview

Class Time: 20 minutes

Prerequisites: Students should have knowledge of the content in Lessons 1.1 through 1.3, specifically:

- an understanding that graphs are read from left to right
- comprehension of the relationship a graph is depicting (In this lesson, the relationship is the idea that population varies as time passes.)
- recognition of whether the dependent variable is increasing or decreasing as the independent variable increases

One of the most important concepts in calculus is *rate of change*. This lesson introduces increasing and decreasing rates of change. Curves with an increasing rate of change are *concave up* (⌣), and curves with a decreasing rate of change are *concave down* (⌢). In calculus, many students have trouble understanding concavity.

 MATH MATTERS

The variable along the *x*-axis is called the *independent variable* and the variable along the *y*-axis is called the *dependent variable*.

 MATH MATTERS

Derivative

The *derivative* gives the instantaneous rate of change of a function and so tells how a function is shifting at a particular point. If the function is describing the relationship between a quantity and time, the derivative can be used to predict what will happen next.

Teaching the Lesson

In students' first semester of calculus, they spend a lot of time *taking the derivative*. The derivative gives the instantaneous rate of change of a function and tells you how a function is shifting at a particular point. If the function is describing the relationship between a quantity and time, the derivative can be used to predict what will happen next. We will not use the terminology but will get a feel for the idea, looking carefully at how the curve changes as we study it, reading from left to right.

All of the questions on the Lesson 1.4 Student Recording Sheet are intended to solicit short answers. Questions 1a through 1c support students in concentrating on the relationship that the graph is describing. All too often, this relationship gets lost when students try to read the points on the graph. It is always important to translate back to the application. (**Note:** Science teachers sometimes express concern that math education does not focus enough on units. The lessons throughout this resource encourage students to think about to what units the numbers correspond.)

Questions 1d and 2a should cause no problem if students have mastered Lessons 1.1 through 1.3. Questions 1e and 2b are the core of the lesson. It may be helpful to ask students "In which city is the population increasing more and more quickly?" and then "In which city is the population increasing more and more slowly?" The short horizontal lines and corresponding vertical lines underneath the curves are in place for learning purposes only.

14 **It's All Connected** The Power of Representation to Build Algebraic Reasoning

The most common misconception is to think if a function is increasing, its rate of change must also be increasing. This is not the case with the population of Stony Creek. In Question 1e, we say "The population is increasing at a decreasing rate." This is a very hard concept for students to grasp. Assure them that they will be revisiting this concept.

If there is time in the lesson, ask students to think in groups about the "Extend the Learning" question.

Homework and Assessment

For homework after finishing the Student Recording Sheet, give students the following three questions. Depending on the general ability and interest level of the class, ask students to draw all three graphs or only one or two of them. You can demonstrate one for additional support. Students should be encouraged to make different choices and instructed to explain their reasoning.

1. Carl ran quickly at first and then slowed down as he became winded. Draw a graph that represents the relationship between distance covered and time. Be sure to label the axes and give the units of measurement.

2. As the radius of a circle gets larger, the area of the circle increases more and more quickly. Draw a graph that represents the relationship between the area and the radius of a circle. Be sure to label the axes and give the units (assuming the radius is measured in inches).

3. As more and more items were produced, the cost per item came down, so the total cost grew more and more slowly. Draw a graph that represents the relationship between the total cost and the number of items produced. Be sure to label the axes and give the units of measurement.

Answers to Lesson 1.4 Student Recording Sheet and Homework

STUDENT RECORDING SHEET

1.
   a. The graph shows the relationship between population and time.
   b. The units of measurement along the x-axis should likely be years. Ask students why it would not make good sense for the unit to be seconds, minutes, days, or weeks.
   c. The units of measurement along the y-axis are numbers of people.
   d. The population is increasing.
   e. The population is increasing by smaller and smaller amounts.

2.
   a. The population is increasing.
   b. The population is increasing by larger and larger amounts. We say "The population is increasing at an increasing rate."

3. Population

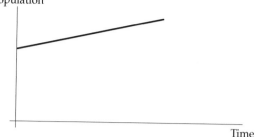

Time

The graph of a function that increases or decreases at a constant rate is said to be *linear*. The population does not start at 0, so the line should not go through the origin. (The *origin* is the point at which the *x*-axis and *y*-axis intersect, which has the coordinates 0,0.)

HOMEWORK

1. Distance

Time

The units along the *x*-axis are minutes and along the *y*-axis, yards.

2. Area

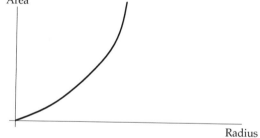

Radius

The units along the *x*-axis are inches and along the *y*-axis, square inches.

Extend the Learning: Describe one situation in which something increases at a constant rate, another situation in which something increases more and more quickly, and a third situation in which something increases more and more slowly.

3. Total cost

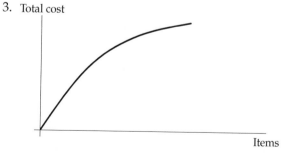

Items

The units along the *x*-axis are items of production and along the *y*-axis, dollars.

Student _____   Class _____   Date _____

LESSON 1.4   Population in Terms of Time
Student Recording Sheet

1. The population of the city of Stony Creek is represented in the graph below.

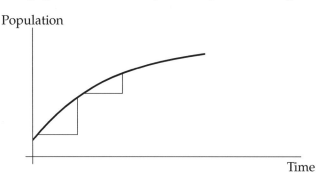

Population

Time

a. This graph shows the relationship between what two quantities?

b. What are the likely units of measurement along the *x*-axis?

c. What are the units of measurement along the *y*-axis?

d. Is the population increasing or decreasing?

e. As time goes by, is the population changing by larger and larger amounts or smaller and smaller amounts? The short horizontal lines underneath the curve are of the same length and so represent two intervals of time of equal length. Study the corresponding changes in population to answer this question.

(continued)

2. The population of the city of Rockville is represented in the graph below.

Population

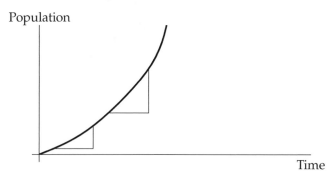

Time

a. Is the population increasing or decreasing?

b. As time goes by, is the population changing by larger and larger amounts or smaller and smaller amounts? The short horizontal lines underneath the curve are of the same length and so represent two intervals of time of equal length. Study the corresponding changes in population to answer this question.

3. The population of the city of Boulder is increasing at a constant rate. In each interval of time, the population increases by the same amount. Draw a graph of the relationship between population and time for Boulder.

Weather in Stony Creek, Rockville, and Boulder

Learn different ways to decrease.

Overview

Class Time: 20 minutes

Prerequisites: Students should have knowledge of the content in Lessons 1.1 through 1.4. Specifically, students should know how to read a graph, understand the relationship a graph is depicting, and recognize whether the dependent variable is increasing or decreasing as the independent variable increases. In addition, students should have covered the content in Lesson 1.4 that looks at increasing functions with differing rates of change.

This lesson introduces increasing and decreasing rates of change for a decreasing function. This can be tricky because if a function is decreasing faster and faster, it is decreasing with a decreasing rate of change. The change is becoming a larger and larger negative number. As the change looks bigger and bigger, students tend to think it is an increasing rate of change. Likewise if it is decreasing more and more slowly, it is decreasing with an increasing rate of change. Since the change looks smaller, students tend to think this is a decreasing rate of change; it is actually an increasing rate of change because it is less negative.

Teaching the Lesson

The concept of increasing and decreasing rates of change for a decreasing function is hard for students to grasp. When completing Lessons 1.4 and 1.5, students may claim they understand what it means to say, "A function is increasing with a decreasing rate of change" or "A function is decreasing with an increasing rate of change." However, in many cases, students do not retain the concept later.

Students' difficulty often stems from two misunderstandings. The first is believing that an increasing function must have an increasing rate of change and that a decreasing function must have a decreasing rate of change. The second misunderstanding involves decreasing functions. For a decreasing function with a decreasing rate of change, students tend to think that the rate of change is increasing because the magnitude of the decrease is getting larger.

Homework and Assessment

Consider assessing students' answers on a 1–3 scale, as shown here.

Assessment Scale

3 Solid answer with good detail

2 Some part of answer incorrect but basic idea understood

1 Some effort made but basic idea not understood

For homework after finishing the Student Recording Sheet, ask students to complete the two following exercises. Both address the notion that when you are moving toward an object, your distance from it gets smaller and smaller.

1.
   a. Graph your distance from school in terms of time, assuming that you are running toward school at a faster and faster rate.
   b. What are the units of measurement along the axes?
2.
   a. Graph your distance from school in terms of time, assuming that you are running toward school at a slower and slower rate.
   b. What are the units of measurement along the axes?

Answers to Lesson 1.5 Student Recording Sheet and Homework

STUDENT RECORDING SHEET

1.
   a. The graph shows the relationship between temperature and time.
   b. The units of measurement along the *x*-axis are likely hours.
   c. The units of measurement along the *y*-axis are degrees.
   d. The temperature is decreasing.
   e. The temperature is decreasing by smaller and smaller amounts. At this point, you may decide to avoid that terminology and just say, "The temperature is decreasing at an increasing rate." Here, we do not use that terminology but say instead that "The temperature is decreasing more and more slowly."
2.
   a. The temperature is decreasing.
   b. The temperature is decreasing by larger and larger amounts. We say, "The temperature is decreasing more and more quickly." Using the more formal terminology, we say, "The temperature is decreasing at a decreasing rate."

3. The graph of a function that increases or decreases at a constant rate is linear.

Temperature

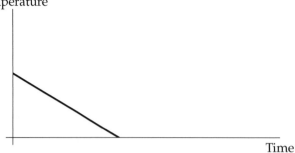

Time

HOMEWORK

1.

a. Distance from school

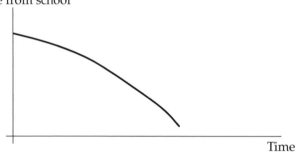

Time

b. Time can be measured in seconds or minutes. Distance can be measured in feet, meters, yards, miles, or kilometers.

2.

a. Distance from school

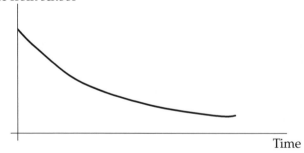

Time

b. Time can be measured in seconds or minutes. Distance can be measured in feet, meters, yards, miles, or kilometers.

Extend the Learning: Discuss how you can tell if a function is increasing or decreasing. If a function is decreasing, how do you know if it is decreasing more and more slowly or more and more quickly? Use both words and illustrations in your explanation.

Student _____ Class _____ Date _____

1. The temperature in the city of Stony Creek during an afternoon is represented in the graph below.

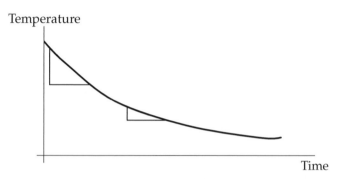

Temperature

Time

a. This graph shows the relationship between what two quantities?

b. What are the likely units of measurement along the x-axis?

c. What are the units of measurement along the y-axis?

d. Is the temperature increasing or decreasing?

e. As time goes by, is the temperature changing by larger and larger amounts or smaller and smaller amounts? The short horizontal lines underneath the curve are of the same length and so represent two intervals of time of equal length. Study the corresponding changes in temperature to answer this question.

(continued)

2. The temperature in the city of Rockville during an afternoon is represented in the graph below.

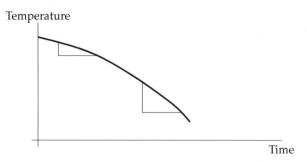

a. Is the temperature increasing or decreasing?

b. As time goes by, is the temperature changing by larger and larger amounts or smaller and smaller amounts? The short horizontal lines underneath the curve are of the same length and so represent two intervals of time of equal length. Study the corresponding changes in temperature to answer this question.

3. The temperature in the city of Boulder is decreasing at a constant rate. In each interval of time, the temperature decreases by the same amount. Draw a graph of the relationship between temperature and time for Boulder.

Owning a Home

Recognize and draw increasing functions with specified rates of change.

Overview

Class Time: 15 minutes

Prerequisites: Students should understand the notion of increasing and decreasing functions and have been introduced to the idea of functions changing more and more slowly or quickly. This content is covered in Lessons 1.4 and 1.5.

In this lesson, students distinguish between increasing functions with differing rates of change. Increasing at a steady rate is exemplified by a straight line and is the easiest to recognize. Students must also identify and then draw a function that increases faster and faster as well as one that increases more and more slowly.

Teaching the Lesson

It is important that students learn to analyze graphs that behave very differently on different intervals. In this lesson, we only cover increasing functions. The content is meant to solidify students' understanding that functions can increase at a decreasing rate, which seems to be the hardest notion for students to absorb.

Homework and Assessment

For homework after finishing the Student Recording Sheet, ask students to complete this problem.

> Your friend tells you that on a trip from his house to the store, he started out walking at a steady pace. Then he ran faster and faster until he was out of breath and had to slow down. Graph his distance from home in terms of time.

Answers to Lesson 1.6 Student Recording Sheet and Homework

STUDENT RECORDING SHEET

1.
   a. Graph I is Hugo's house, Graph II is Mary's house, and Graph III is Chris's house.

b. The units of measurement along the horizontal axis are years.

c. The units of measurement along the vertical axis are dollars.

2.

a. George's walk

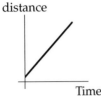

Nick's walk

Suzanna's walk

b. The units of measurement for the *x*-axis are likely seconds or minutes or possibly hours. The units of measurement for the *y*-axis are likely feet, yards, or miles.

HOMEWORK

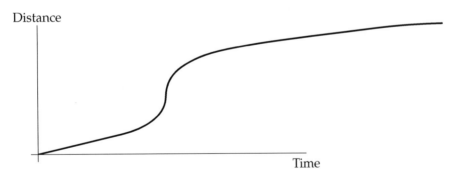

> **Extend the Learning:** Instead of graphing *distance* in terms of time, you could graph *speed* in terms of time. What would that graph look like?
>
> **Answer:** The graph would be constant, then increase, and then decrease.

LESSON **1.6** **Owning a Home**
Student Recording Sheet

1. Suppose the value of real estate is increasing in the city of Lakeville. The value of Chris's house is rising at a constant rate. Each year, the value of his house increases by the same amount. The value of Hugo's house is increasing more and more quickly. Each year, the increase in value is bigger than the increase of the previous year. The value of Mary's house is going up but more and more slowly. Each year, the value of her house increases by an amount that is smaller than the increase of the previous year.

   a. Look at the graphs below. Decide which graph corresponds to the value of Chris's house, to the value of Hugo's house, and to the value of Mary's house.

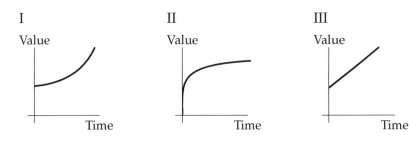

   b. What are the units of measurement along the horizontal axis?

   c. What are the units of measurement along the vertical axis?

2. George, Nick, and Suzanna are each walking away from home. George is walking at a steady pace, Nick is walking faster and faster, and Suzanna is slowing down the longer she walks.

   a. Graph the relationship between distance from home and time for each walker. Use the graphs above to help you draw the appropriate curves.

   b. Be sure to label the axes. What are the most likely units of measurement for the *x*-axis? What are the most likely units of measurement for the *y*-axis?

From *It's All Connected: The Power of Representation to Build Algebraic Reasoning, Grades 6–9* by Frances Van Dyke. © 2012 by Scholastic Inc. Permission granted to photocopy for nonprofit use in a classroom or similar place dedicated to face-to-face educational purposes. Downloadable at www.mathsolutions.com/itsallconnectedalgebrarereproducibles.

Cars and Walking to School

Recognize and draw decreasing functions with specified rates of change.

Overview

Class Time: 15 minutes

Prerequisites: Students should understand decreasing functions and have been introduced to the idea of functions decreasing more and more quickly or slowly. This content is covered in Lessons 1.4 and 1.5.

In this lesson, students distinguish between decreasing functions with differing rates of change. Like the case for increasing functions, decreasing at a steady rate is exemplified by a straight line and is the easiest to recognize. Students must also identify and then draw a function that decreases faster and faster as well one that decreases more and more slowly.

Teaching the Lesson

In this lesson, only decreasing functions are considered. The content is meant to solidify students' understanding that functions can decrease at an increasing rate.

Homework and Assessment

For homework after finishing the Student Recording Sheet, ask each student to draw a graph of a decreasing function for which the rate of decrease changes. Also have each student write a sentence that describes the graph.

Answers to Lesson 1.7 Student Recording Sheet and Homework

STUDENT RECORDING SHEET

1.
   a. Graph I corresponds to the value of Fatima's car, Graph II corresponds to the value of Kate's car, and Graph III corresponds to the value of Jeff's car.
   b. The units of measurement along the *x*-axis are years.
   c. The units of measurement along the *y*-axis are dollars.

2.

a. Juan's walk to school

Distance from school

Time

Carlo's walk to school

Distance from school

Time

Martha's walk to school

Distance from school

Time

b. The units of measurement along the *x*-axis could be seconds or minutes. The units of measurement along the *y*-axis could be feet or miles.

HOMEWORK

Answers will vary. As an example, if the student says the function decreases first at a steady rate and then faster and faster, the graph must reflect that, looking like the following.

Extend the Learning: Look at the following graph:

Distance

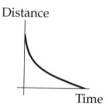

Time

We say a graph shaped like this is "Decreasing with an increasing rate of change." Can you explain why?

Answer: The change is becoming less negative, so it indicates an increase.

Cars and Walking to School

Student Recording Sheet

1. The value of a car decreases after it has been purchased. The value of Jeff's Honda is decreasing at a constant rate. Each year, the value of his car decreases by the same amount. The value of Fatima's Ford is decreasing more and more quickly. Each year, the decrease in value is bigger than the decrease of the previous year. The value of Kate's Volvo is going down but more and more slowly. Each year, the value of her car decreases by a smaller amount than the decrease of the previous year.

   a. Look at the graphs below. Decide which graph corresponds to the value of Jeff's car, to the value of Fatima's car, and to the value of Kate's car.

   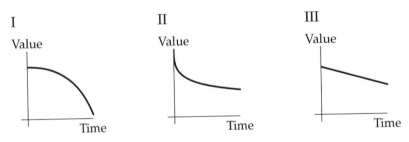

   b. What are the units of measurement along the x-axis?

   c. What are the units of measurement along the y-axis?

2. Juan, Carlo, and Martha are walking toward the school. Juan is walking at a steady pace, Carlo is walking faster and faster, and Martha is slowing down as she walks.

   a. For each walker, graph the relationship between the distance from school and time. Use the graphs below to help you draw the appropriate curves.

   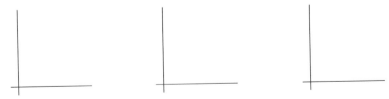

   b. Be sure to label the axes. What are the units of measurement for the x-axis? What are the units of measurement for the y-axis?

Distance and Population

Recognize and draw graphs with specified rates of change.

Overview

Class Time: 20 minutes

Prerequisites: Students should have completed Lessons 1.1 through 1.5.

Here for the first time both increasing and decreasing functions with varying rates of change are considered in the same lesson. If you feel the students have mastered the notion of differing rates, you may want to skip this lesson and go on to Lesson 1.9.

Teaching the Lesson

This lesson provides an exercise to come back to if students forget what it means for an increasing function to have a decreasing rate of change or for a decreasing function to have an increasing rate of change.

Homework and Assessment

For homework after finishing the Student Recording Sheet, ask students to complete these problems:

1. The senator said, "We have reached a crucial moment. Our debt is still increasing, but until now, it has been increasing at an increasing rate. Now, it is starting to increase at a decreasing rate." Draw a graph of debt in terms of time that represents the senator's statement.
2. The mayor said, "We have really turned things around. The population of our city used to decrease faster and faster. Then it began to decrease slower and slower, and now, it is increasing at a steady pace." Draw a graph of population in terms of time that represents the mayor's statement.

Answers to Lesson 1.8 Student Recording Sheet and Homework

STUDENT RECORDING SHEET

1.
   a. Graph I represents Gail's walk, Graph II represents Kim's walk, and Graph III represents Janet's walk. Discuss that in Graph I, as time passes, more and more distance is covered in a unit of time. In Graph II, the opposite is true: As time passes, less and less distance is covered in an equal interval of time. In Graph III, equal amounts of distance are covered in equal intervals of time.

b. The graphs show the relationship between distance and time.

c. The units of measurement for the *x*-axis are likely seconds, or minutes rather than hours. The people are walking away from a field. This is accomplished in minutes or seconds rather than hours. The units of measurement for the *y*-axis are likely feet, meters, or yards rather than miles. The act of walking away from a field invokes the idea of a short distance accomplished in a short time.

2.

a. Graph I represents the population of Plasterburg, Graph II represents the population of Bricksville, and Graph III represents the population of Stonetown. Discuss how (moving from left to right) allowing time to pass changes the drop in population in Graphs I and III but not in Graph II.

b. The units of measurement are years along the *x*-axis. The units of measurement are the number of people along the *y*-axis. When you are considering the growth of a population in a city, it makes sense to look at change occurring after years rather than months or days.

3. Here is a possible answer:

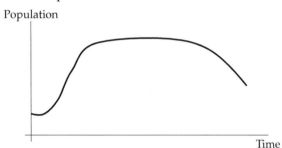

HOMEWORK

1.

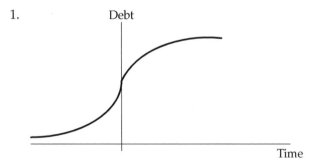

2. Population

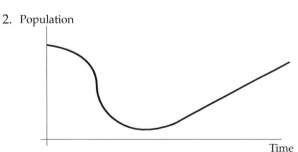

Extend the Learning: Write a sentence to describe the following graph:

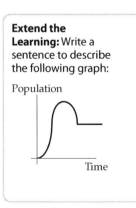

Student _____ Class _____ Date _____

1. Janet, Gail, and Kim all walked away from the field. Janet walked at a steady pace, Gail sped up as she walked, and Kim slowed down.

   a. Look at the graphs below. Then decide which graph represents each girl's walk.

   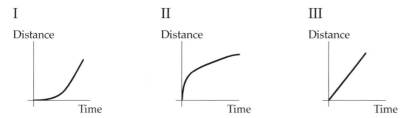

   I   Distance / Time
   II   Distance / Time
   III   Distance / Time

   b. The graphs show the relationship between what two quantities?

   c. What are the likely units of measurement along the axes? Explain your answers.

2. The population of Bricksville is decreasing at a steady rate. The population of Stone-town is decreasing at a faster and faster rate. The population of Plasterburg is decreasing but at a slower and slower rate.

   a. Look at the graphs below. Then decide which graph represents each town's population.

   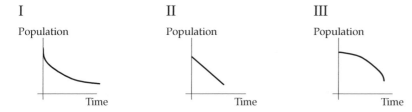

   I   Population / Time
   II   Population / Time
   III   Population / Time

   b. What are the likely units of measurement along the axes? Explain your answers.

3. The population of Bristol increased rapidly at first and then more and more slowly until it stopped growing. It remained the same for awhile, and then it began to decrease.

   Draw a graph of the population of Bristol in terms of time.

From *It's All Connected: The Power of Representation to Build Algebraic Reasoning, Grades 6–9* by Frances Van Dyke. © 2012 by Scholastic Inc. Permission granted to photocopy for nonprofit use in a classroom or similar place dedicated to face-to-face educational purposes. Downloadable at www.mathsolutions.com/itsallconnectedalgebrareproducibles.

An Antique, a Jewel, and a Car

Compare and contrast values; create multiple graphs on one set of axes.

Overview

Class Time: 25 minutes

Prerequisites: Students should have completed Lessons 1.1 through 1.4.

This lesson has students compare and contrast three graphs all graphed on the same set of axes. This is the first time more than one relationship has been graphed on a single set of axes.

Teaching the Lesson

In previous lessons, students have focused on a single graph on each set of axes. Here, they are asked to look at three graphs from both a local and a global point of view. This ties together the content learned thus far in Section I.

Homework and Assessment

For homework after finishing the Student Recording Sheet, ask students to complete this problem:

> The graph below records the average prices of homes in terms of time since the year 2000 for three different towns. Time is graphed along the *x*-axis, and price is graphed along the *y*-axis. Study the graph and answer the questions.

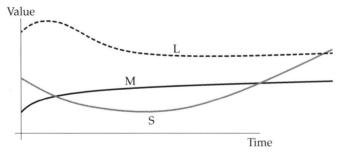

1. Make up names for the three towns that start with the three letters on the graph:

   L _____

   M _____

   S _____

2. For each town, describe what has happened to the average price of a home over time.
3. Compare and contrast the prices of homes in the three towns over time.

Answers to Lesson 1.9 Student Recording Sheet and Homework

STUDENT RECORDING SHEET

1.
    a. The graph shows the relationship between value and time.
    b. The units of measurement along the horizontal axis should be years, because we think of the value of these objects as changing over a long period of time.
    c. The units of measurement along the vertical axis should be dollars.
    d. The jewel is increasing in value.
    e. The car is decreasing in value.
    f. The value of the antique is not changing.
    g. The car starts off having the highest value.
    h. The jewel ends up having the highest value.
    i. The antique starts off having the lowest value.
    j. The car ends up having the lowest value.
    k. The jewel's value does not change at a constant rate. It changes at a slower and slower rate as time goes by.

2.
    a. Value

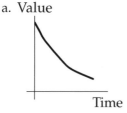

    b. The units of measurement should be time in years for the horizontal axis and value in dollars for the vertical axis.

HOMEWORK

1. Answers will vary. The names of the three towns should start with the three letters on the graph—for example, Lanesboro, Marshall, and Stockton.
2. In Town L, the average price of a home first rose and then fell more and more slowly until it became constant. In Town M, the average price of a home rose but more and more slowly until it became constant. In Town S, the average price of a home fell more and more slowly until it began to rise again. In 2000, the average price of a home in Town L was higher than that of a home in Town S, which was higher than the price of a home in Town M.
3. At present, the average price of a home in Town S is slightly above that of a home in Town L and significantly above that of a home in Town M.

Extend the Learning: Make up a graphing problem of the type you solved in this lesson. Describe a situation in which three separate items change in value over time, and explain how they change. Then draw three graphs on one set of axes that correspond to your situation and explanation. Also create five questions about your graphs, and provide their answers.

LESSON 1.9 An Antique, a Jewel, and a Car
Student Recording Sheet

1. The following graph records the value of an object in terms of time for three differ-ent objects. The objects are an antique, a car, and a jewel. Each curve is labeled with the first letter of the object to which it corresponds: A for antique, C for car, and J for jewel. Time is graphed along the *x*-axis, and value is graphed along the *y*-axis. Study the graph and answer the questions.

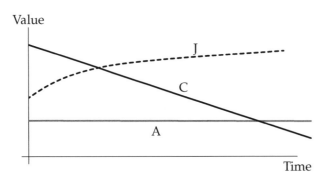

   a. This graph shows a relationship between which two quantities?

   b. What should be the units of measurement along the horizontal axis?

   c. What should be the units of measurement along the vertical axis?

   d. Which object is increasing in value?

   e. Which object is decreasing in value?

(continued)

f. Which object's value is not changing?

g. Which object starts off having the highest value?

h. Which object ends up having the highest value?

i. Which object starts off having the lowest value?

j. Which object ends up having the lowest value?

k. Which object's value does not change at a constant rate? How does its value change?

2. The value of a car decreases over time but more and more slowly.

a. Draw a graph that represents the value of a car in terms of time.

b. What should be the units of measurement for the horizontal and vertical axes?

Distance to a Bench

Compare and contrast linear graphs.

Overview

Class Time: 25 minutes

Prerequisites: Students should have completed Lessons 1.1 through 1.3 and 1.9.

In this lesson, students compare and contrast three different people's positions from a bench in terms of time. This lesson is quite a bit harder than Lesson 1.9, which should be done before attempting this one.

Teaching the Lesson

Students need to realize that people can stand on different sides of something and not have to cross each other when they move toward it or away from it. Thus, students need to resist saying that people are together when the curves intersect. The temptation to do this is very strong. The teacher should ask if it is possible for people to be at an equal distance from an object but nowhere near each other. This exercise can be replicated in the classroom with a chair and two students standing and moving on different sides of it.

 MATH MATTERS

Curves

It is standard practice for mathematicians to refer to *lines* as *curves*. This language is sometimes troubling for students and may need reinforcement.

Homework and Assessment

For homework after finishing the Student Recording Sheet, ask students to complete the following problems:

1. Look at the graph below. It shows the distance of a train and a bus from a particular station.

a. Which is arriving at the station? Which is leaving the station? Explain your answers.

b. Do the train and the bus necessarily have to pass each other? Explain your answer.

c. Which is going faster? Explain your answer.

2. The graph below records three different people's positions from a beach in terms of time. Time is graphed along the x-axis, and distance is graphed along the y-axis. Study the graph and answer the questions.

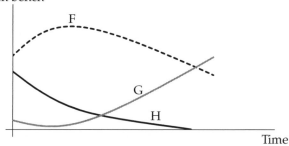

Distance from bench

Time

a. Give the three people names that start with the three letters on the graph:

F _____

G _____

H _____

b. Describe each person's position in terms of the beach over time. Also talk about each person's speed.

c. Compare and contrast the positions of the three people over time.

Answers to Lesson 1.10 Student Recording Sheet and Homework

STUDENT RECORDING SHEET

1.

a. Answers will vary. The names of the three people should start with the three letters on the graph—for example, Emma, Foster, and Grady.

b. This graph shows the relationship between time and distance.

c. The units of measurement along the x-axis are likely seconds.

d. The units of measurement along the y-axis are likely feet or meters.

e. Person E is walking toward the bench.

f. Person F is walking away from the bench.

g. Person G is maintaining the same distance from the bench and so could be standing still or even circling it.

h. Person E starts off farthest from the bench.

i. Person E walks most quickly. The slope of Curve E is the steepest of the three curves, which means a greater amount of distance is being covered in a shorter amount of time.

j. Person E reaches the bench. His or her distance from the bench goes down to 0.

k. Yes, the three people are moving at constant rates, as the curves are linear.

l. Person E and Person F could be on different sides of the bench. In that case, they would not have to pass each other.

2.

HOMEWORK

1.
    a. The train is arriving at the station. The bus is leaving the station. As time passes, the train's distance from the station decreases while that of the bus increases.
    b. The train and the bus do not necessarily have to pass each other. They could be running on opposite sides of the station.
    c. The train is going faster. On the graph, its curve has a steeper slope, which indicates that it covers more distance than the bus in an equal interval of time.

2.
    a. Answers will vary. The names of the three people should start with the three letters on the graph—for example, Faith, Gabe, and Hallie.
    b. Person F first walked away from the beach, walking slower and slower, and then walked toward the beach. Person G first walked toward the beach, walking slower and slower, and then walked away from the beach. Person H walked toward the beach, slowing down but then reaching the beach.
    c. At the start of the walk, Person F was farthest from the beach and Person G was closest to the beach. At the end of the walk, Person H was at the beach and Person G was farthest from the beach.

> **Extend the Learning:** Explain why a steeper slope on a graph showing distance versus time indicates a faster speed.

Student _____ Class _____ Date _____

1. The graph below records three different people's positions from a bench in terms of time. Time is graphed along the *x*-axis, and distance is graphed along the *y*-axis. Study the graph and answer the questions.

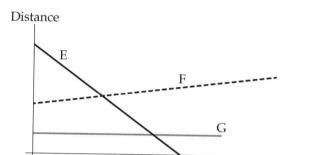

a. Give the three people names that start with the three letters on the graph:

E _____

F _____

G _____

b. This graph shows the relationship between which two quantities?

c. What are the likely units of measurement along the *x*-axis?

d. What are the likely units of measurement along the *y*-axis?

e. Who is walking toward the bench?

f. Who is walking away from the bench?

(continued)

From *It's All Connected: The Power of Representation to Build Algebraic Reasoning, Grades 6–9* by Frances Van Dyke. © 2012 by Scholastic Inc.
Permission granted to photocopy for nonprofit use in a classroom or similar place dedicated to face-to-face educational purposes.
Downloadable at www.mathsolutions.com/itsallconnectedalgebrareproducibles.

g. Who might be standing still?

h. Who starts off farthest from the bench?

i. Who walks most quickly? How can you tell?

j. Who reaches the bench? How can you tell?

k. Are the three people moving at constant rates? How can you tell?

l. Person E and Person F do not necessarily have to pass each other. Explain how.

2. Draw a graph that records the position of another person, Kate, from the bench in terms of time. Kate is moving toward the bench. She walks quickly at first and then more and more slowly.

At the Beach

Compare and contrast distance-versus-time graphs.

Overview

Class Time: 25 minutes

Prerequisites: Students should have completed Lessons 1.1 through 1.3 and 1.10.

In this lesson, students compare and contrast three different people's positions from a beach in terms of time. This lesson is similar to Lesson 1.10 but considers varying rates of change.

Teaching the Lesson

As in Lesson 1.10, students need to recognize that people can be standing on different sides of an object and do not necessarily have to cross each other when they move toward it or away from it. And again, students need to avoid the temptation to say that people are together when the curves intersect. A class demonstration involving two students and a chair can help clarify these concepts.

Homework and Assessment

For homework after finishing the Student Recording Sheet, ask students to analyze the following, which shows a distance-versus-time graph for three individuals A, B, and C walking from home to school.

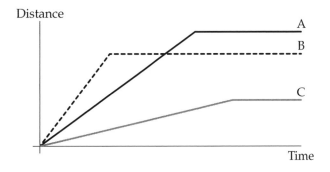

Write a few sentences describing and comparing the trips of A, B, and C to school.

Include who lived farthest, who lived closest, who got to school first, who got there last, who walked the fastest and who walked most slowly.

STUDENT RECORDING SHEET

1.
   a. Answers will vary. The names of the three people should start with the three letters on the graph—for example, Frankie, Grace, and Hannah.
   b. Person F first walked away from the beach, walking slower and slower, and then walked toward the beach. Person G first walked toward the beach, walking slower and slower, and then walked away from the beach. Person H walked toward the beach, slowing down and then reaching the beach.
   c. At the beginning of the walk, Person F was farthest from the beach and Person G was closest to the beach. At the end of the walk, Person H was at the beach and Person G was farthest from the beach.

HOMEWORK

Possible answer: Everyone walked at a steady pace. C lived closest, walked the most slowly, and got there last. B lived farther away from school than C but not as far as A. He or she walked the fastest and got there first. A lived farthest from school walked faster than C and got there before C.

Explanation of possible answer: The horizontal lines indicate the distance is no longer changing so they are at school. The corresponding level at which the horizontal line starts on the vertical axis indicates the distance traveled. The corresponding level at which the horizontal line starts on the horizontal axis indicates the time taken to get to school. The slope of the line segment from the origin to the horizontal line represents the speed. The steeper the line the more distance is covered in the same unit of time.

Student _____ Class _____ Date _____

1. The graph below records three different people's positions in terms of time. Time is graphed along the horizontal axis, and distance from a beach is graphed along the vertical axis. Study the graph and answer the questions.

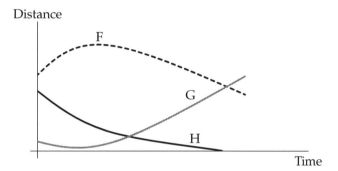

a. Give the three people names that start with the three letters on the graph:

F   _____

G   _____

H   _____

b. Describe each person's position in terms of the beach over time. Also talk about each person's speed.

c. Compare and contrast the positions of the three people over time.

Value, Population, and Distance over Time

Practice writing sentences describing graphs.

1.A FURTHER PRACTICE

Overview

Class or Homework Time: 15 minutes

Prerequisites: Students should have completed Lessons 1.1 and 1.2.

This lesson looks again at writing sentences that describe what is represented on graphs. This concept should be reviewed if students need additional work for mastery.

Teaching the Lesson

The lesson can be assigned as homework, done in class, or split between the two (perhaps one question done in class and the others assigned as homework).

Answers to Further Practice 1.A Student Recording Sheet

Answers will vary, but students' sentences should compare changes as time passed.

Student _____ Class _____ Date _____

For each graph, write a sentence that describes what it represents. Begin each sentence with the phrase *As time passed*. In writing about Graphs 1 and 2, choose objects whose value is changing with time. In writing about Graph 3, make up the name of a place whose population is changing with time. In writing about Graph 4, choose a setting for the problem.

1. Graph 1

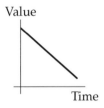

_____

_____

2. Graph 2

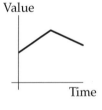

_____

_____

(continued)

3. Graph 3

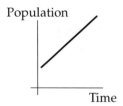

_____

_____

4. Graph 4

_____

_____

Your Choice and Animals at the Zoo

Practice rates of change with increasing functions.

Overview

Class or Homework Time: 20 minutes

Prerequisites: Students should have completed Lessons 1.1 through 1.5.

This lesson looks again at increasing functions with different rates of change. This concept should be reviewed if students need additional work for mastery.

Teaching the Lesson

The lesson can be assigned as homework, done in class, or split between the two (perhaps one question done in class and the others assigned as homework). Students tend to grasp the concept of increasing functions with a decreasing rate of change and claim to understand it but then lose it over time. This lesson can be used for review if that is the case in your classroom.

Answers to Further Practice 1.B Student Recording Sheet

1. Answers will vary. The words *at a constant rate* should be used in the sentence about Graph III. The words *slower and slower* should be used in the sentence about Graph II. The words *faster and faster* should be used in the sentence about Graph I.

2. For all three graphs, the *x*-axis should be labeled *Pounds* and the *y*-axis should be labeled *Months*.

Monkey

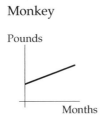

Wolf

Panda

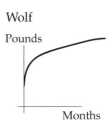

Student _____ Class _____ Date _____

Your Choice and Animals at the Zoo
Student Recording Sheet

1. Look at the following three graphs. For each graph, write a sentence that describes it. In each case, be sure to label the axes and give the units of measurement. One of your descriptive sentences should include the words *at a constant rate*, another should include the words *slower and slower*, and the third should include the words *faster and faster*. Decide which words fit which graph.

Graph I   Graph II   Graph III

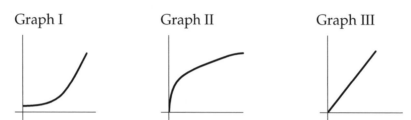

2. Three animals at the zoo are putting on weight. A monkey is gaining weight at a steady rate. As each month passes, it gains about the same amount of weight. A panda is gaining weight at a faster and faster rate. It is getting heavier and heavier as time goes by. A wolf is gaining weight but more and more slowly. On the axes, draw a graph of each animal's weight gain. Be sure to label the axes.

Monkey   Panda   Wolf

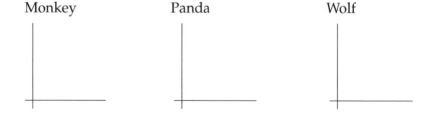

Make Your Own Example

Practice with varying rates of change.

Overview

Class or Homework Time: 20 minutes

Prerequisites: Students should have completed Lessons 1.1 through 1.8.

This lesson looks again at writing sentences that describe graphs with varying rates of change. This concept should be reviewed if students need additional work for mastery.

Teaching the Lesson

The lesson can be assigned as homework, done in class, or split between the two (perhaps one question done in class and the others assigned as homework).

Answers to Further Practice 1.C Student Recording Sheet

Answers will vary.
1. Make sure student mentions as quantity along x-axis increases, quantity along y-axis increases more and more rapidly.
2. Make sure student mentions as quantity along x-axis increases, quantity along y-axis decreases but more and more slowly.
3. Make sure student mentions as quantity along x-axis increases, quantity along y-axis increases also but more and more slowly.
4. Make sure student mentions as quantity along x-axis increases, quantity along y-axis decreases at a constant rate.
5. Make sure student mentions as quantity along x-axis increases, quantity along y-axis decreases more and more rapidly
6. Make sure student mentions as quantity along x-axis increases, quantity along y-axis increases at a constant rate.

Student _____ Class _____ Date _____

Make Your Own Example
Student Recording Sheet

For each graph below, write a sentence that describes what it represents. Be sure to label the axes and accurately describe the relationship between the two quantities.

1. Graph 1

_____

_____

_____

_____

2. Graph 2

_____

_____

_____

_____

3. Graph 3

_____

_____

_____

_____

4. Graph 4

_____

_____

_____

_____

(continued)

5. Graph 5

_____

_____

_____

_____

6. Graph 6

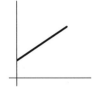

_____

_____

_____

_____

Quantitative Graphs

Overview

In this section, the lessons focus on graphs that are quantitative and have possibly different scales along both axes. The section begins with a lesson in which students must determine the scales along the axes with no particular application in mind. Next, students complete a lesson in which the application determines the scales. After points are added to the graph, students are asked to consider details of the relationship portrayed in addition to the overall trend. All of the relationships are functions, so each value of x is assigned to only one value of y. Given a specific value of x, students are asked to find y, and given a specific value of y, they are asked to find x. Throughout high school, students will be asked this type of question.

For particular points on a curve, students are asked to write descriptive sentences in terms of the application using the information provided by the coordinates of the points. Supplied with information about the application, students must locate the corresponding point on the graph. As in Section I, students continue to be asked how the functions are changing.

Lessons

LESSON 2.1   **Numbers on a Line**   *56*
Estimate points and tick marks along axes given certain values.

LESSON 2.2   **Height of a Person**   *60*
Estimate scales along axes given height as a function of time.

LESSON 2.3   **Value of a Car**   *65*
Read and interpret a quantitative graph of a decreasing function.

LESSON 2.4   **Rising Real Estate Prices**   *68*
Interpret a quantitative graph of an increasing function with a decreasing rate of change.

LESSON 2.5   **Perimeter of a Square**   *71*
Use the graph of the linear function $y = 4x$.

LESSON 2.6   **Area of a Square**   *76*
Use the graph of the quadratic function $y = x^2$.

LESSON 2.7   **A Rumor in the Classroom**   *81*
Interpret a graph with a point of inflection.

LESSON 2.8   **Using a Motion Detector**   *85*
Interpret a quantitative graph of a decreasing function with a decreasing rate of change.

LESSON 2.9   **Mark's Distance from the Cafeteria**   *90*
Work with a distance-versus-time graph.

LESSON 2.10   **Value of a Boat**   *95*
Work with a decreasing function with an increasing rate of change.

LESSON 2.11   **Rocket in the Air**   *100*
Work with a quadratic function that models the height of a rocket in terms of time.

LESSON 2.12   **Beehive Rocket**   *103*
Draw the path of a rocket.

Numbers on a Line

Estimate points and tick marks along axes given certain values.

Overview

Class Time: 20 minutes

Prerequisites: Students should have some experience locating points on the *xy* (Cartesian) plane.

In this lesson, students practice looking at different unit lengths along the axes and identifying the proper locations of points. Examples of these problems can be worked through on the board before students complete the Student Recording Sheet.

Teaching the Lesson

The lessons in this section present graphs on which the axes will have scales and we will put points on our graphs. In many applications, the unit length along the *x*-axis is very different from the unit length along the *y*-axis. An example of this is seen in Lesson 2.4, where students look at the value of a car in terms of years since purchase. This exercise gives students practice looking at different unit lengths along the axes and giving the proper point location that results. Examples of these problems can be given on the board before the students tackle the sheet. Start by using a single number line. Place the 0 and unit and then ask students to place different values, say 4 and –2, being careful to take the unit length into account. Try a second number line below your first placing 0 directly below its counterpart but this time have a different length for your unit. Get students to represent 4 and –2 in this case and explain the disparity. This exercise can be repeated if necessary. Next try a number line on which just 0 and 2 are marked. Discuss how to locate 5. (You might advise them to locate the unit and use that, although some will want to look at 2.5 times the length for 2.) Do more exercises of this type and then do the same thing on a pair of coordinate axes.

Homework and Assessment

For homework after finishing the recording sheet, ask each student to make up a problem of the type covered in this lesson to give to a classmate. The student should provide a solution to the problem, as well.

STUDENT RECORDING SHEET

1. To locate 3 along the *x*-axis, look at the unit length (which is indicated by the placement of 1) and then triple it. To locate –3 along the *x*-axis, move the same distance from the origin but on the other side of the *y*-axis. Similarly, to locate 3 along the *y*-axis, triple the length of 1 unit along that axis. To locate –3, move the same distance from the origin but below the *x*-axis.

2. To determine the length of 1 unit, take one-fifth the distance from the origin to 5 along the *x*-axis. Then triple that unit length to locate 3. Locate –3 along the *x*-axis by moving the same distance from the origin but on the other side of the *y*-axis. Similarly, to locate 3 along the *y*-axis, determine 1 unit length for that axis and then triple it. Locate –3 along the *y*-axis by moving the same distance from the origin but below the *x*-axis.

3. Lightly sketch vertical lines through 3 and –3 on the *x*-axis. Then sketch horizontal lines through 3 and –3 on the *y*-axis. Extend the lines far enough so that they connect, forming a rectangle. The corners of the rectangle give you the four desired points.

HOMEWORK

Answers will vary. Each problem should involve determining and then applying units of scale along both axes, and each solution should involve a correct explanation of how to solve the problem as was done in the problems above.

Extend the Learning: Explain why the following choice of axes makes sense if you wish graph the value of a car in terms of years since purchase. (Answer: A car may be $30000 when purchased and decline in value to a few thousand dollars after 10 years. Along the *x*-axis it makes sense to have units from 1 to 10, whereas along the *y*-axis you need to show thousands.)

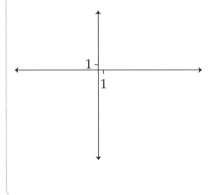

(continued)

What scales would you use along the axes if you wanted to graph a man's weight in pounds in terms of his age in years? You may assume he lives to be 80 and never weighs over 300 pounds.

Student _____ Class _____ Date _____

1. Locate 3 and –3 along the *x*-axis and then along the *y*-axis. Mark each location with a tick mark on the axis. Explain the process you used to determine each location.

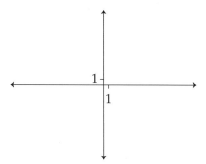

2. Note the placement of 5 along the *x*-axis and then along the *y*-axis. Then mark the approximate locations of 3 and –3 along each axis. Again, explain the process you used to determine each location.

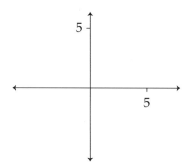

3. Put the points (3,–3), (3,3), (–3,3) and (–3,–3) on each graph.

Height of a Person

Estimate scales along axes given height as a function of time.

Overview

Class Time: 15 minutes

Prerequisites: Students should have completed Lessons 1.1 through 1.3 and 2.1.

In this lesson, students are asked again to determine the proper scales along the axes. However, this time, the scales are determined by the application.

Teaching the Lesson

Students should have a basic understanding of how a person's height changes over time and how to depict that relationship. The day before doing the lesson, ask students to think about the relationship between growth and age. To ensure students' understanding, discuss the concept in class.

Homework and Assessment

For homework after finishing the recording sheet, ask each student to produce a graph that represents a person's weight in terms of time. Also ask each student to explain his or her answer, describing the different parts of the graph. This carries on the extended learning question from Lesson 2.1.

Answers to Lesson 2.2 Student Recording Sheet and Homework

 MATH MATTERS

y-**Intercept**
The y-intercept is the place on the graph where the curve hits the y-axis.

STUDENT RECORDING SHEET

1. The correct answer is Graph D. A man's height is about 2 feet at birth and then increases during his first 20 years to 6 feet on average. After that, it stays the same for most of his life but decreases slightly at the end. On the graph, this is shown by the curve beginning at the *y*-intercept of 2. The man's growth to 6 feet during his first 20 years can be traced along the *x*-axis, as can his maintaining that height for most of his life but shrinking slightly at the end.

The horizontal axis should be labeled *Time*, and the units of measurement should be *years*. The scale should be shown in twenty-year intervals. The vertical axis should be labeled *Height*, and the units of measurement should be *feet*. The scale should be shown in 2-foot intervals.

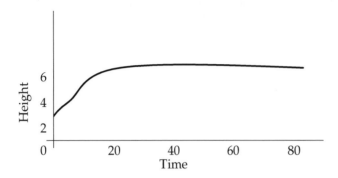

2. The *y*-intercept represents the man's starting height (or his length at birth).
   The two graphs will have the same axes labels and units of measurement (*Time* and *years* for the *x*-axis, and *Height* and *feet* for the *y*-axis.) The two graphs will also have similar shapes, showing the trend of increasing height, then maintaining height, and then slightly decreasing height. However, the *x*-values will end at 60 years, and the *y*-values will be lower than the graph shown in D. Here is a possible answer.

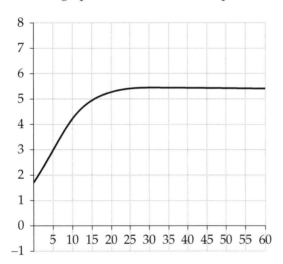

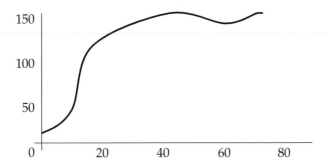

Students' graphs representing weight are more likely to vary than those representing height, as various factors can affect a person's weight across a lifetime (e.g., dieting, fitness level, illness, etc.).

Extend the Learning: To be a function, only one height value must be possible for each weight value. It is possible for a person to weigh the same amount at two different heights.

Answer: If we look at a person's height in relation to his or her weight, our result may not be a function. Why?

Student ______________________ Class __________________ Date ______________

LESSON 2.2 Height of a Person

Student Recording Sheet

1. A man died when he was 80 years old. Which of the graphs below likely represents his height over his lifetime? Explain your reasoning. Also label the axes and give the units of measurement and scale.

To get started, label the axes and give the units of measurement and scale. Along the horizontal axis, which represents age, estimate where 20 is. Mark it, and then estimate the locations of 40, 60, and 80. Along the vertical axis, which represents height, estimate where 6 is. (Assume the average height of a 40-year-old man is about 6 feet.) Mark it, and then estimate the locations of 2 and 4 feet.

Graph A

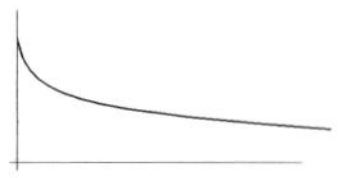

Graph B

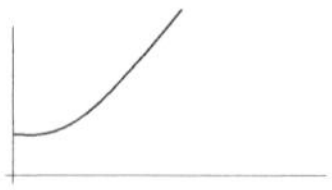

Graph C

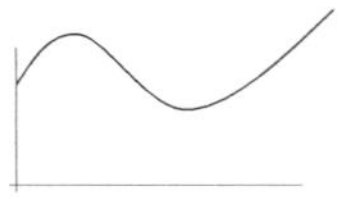

Graph D

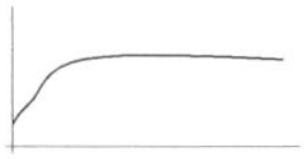

2. The *y*-intercept is the place on the graph where the curve hits the *y*-axis. What does it represent in this problem about a man's height?

3. Draw the graph of the height over a lifetime for a woman who dies at age 60. Compare and contrast this graph with the one you chose as your answer to Question 1.

Value of a Car

Read and interpret a quantitative graph of a decreasing function.

Overview

Class Time: 20 minutes

Prerequisites: Students should have completed Lessons 1.1 through 1.5.

In this lesson, students translate values and points into the context of an application. This is at the heart of interpreting and learning from a graphical representation.

Teaching the Lesson

First, conduct this lesson orally as a class, and then have students write the answers on their own. No single question is very difficult, but translating values and points into meaningful sentences about the application takes practice. Standard questions to ask about graphs include "Given x, what is y?" and "Given y, what is x?" Both questions are introduced here in the context of the value of a car in relation to the number of years since its purchase.

The idea of value decreasing more and more slowly is also addressed in this lesson, and it will require students to remember this concept from Lesson 1.5. You may want to look at Lesson 1.5 again and briefly review the concept before doing this lesson.

Homework and Assessment

For homework after finishing the recording sheet, ask students to solve this problem: Look again at the graph in the recording sheet. Write a paragraph describing the relationship between the value of the car and the years since it was purchased. Include details that were not included in the questions on the recording sheet. In particular, choose two points on the curve and write sentences about the information they provide.

STUDENT RECORDING SHEET

1.
   a. The graph shows the relationship between time and value.
   b. The units of measurement along the horizontal axis are likely years. (When introducing this lesson to students, talk about tracking the value of a car over years. Otherwise, some students may think that the appropriate units of measurement are days, hours, or minutes. Also mention that the value of a car drops dramatically in the beginning.)
   c. The units of measurement along the vertical axis are likely dollars. (Often, students answer "Money." Try to get them to recognize that money is measured in units, such as dollars.)
   d. The car is decreasing in value. (A typical student answer is "It goes down." Encourage students to write a more complete answer: "As time passes, the value of the car is decreasing" or "As we move from left to right along the x-axis, the curve is falling, which shows a decrease in the car's value.")
   e. The car's value is changing at a slower and slower rate. Students have a hard time explaining why this is so. Encourage them to see that as time passes, the value decreases more and more slowly. When moving from left to right along the x-axis, equal intervals of time correspond with smaller and smaller drops in value.)
   f. After 6 years, the value of the car is about $9,000. (Discuss the information provided by several other points if students have a hard time answering this question.)
   g. One year after purchase, the car is worth $24,000.
   h. The car is worth $12,000 after approximately 4½ years. (Encourage students to write complete sentences with reference to time and value. They tend to provide only numbers.)
   i. The y-intercept indicates that the car was purchased for $30,000.

HOMEWORK

Answers will vary.

> **Extend the Learning:** Find a graph about two real-world quantities in a newspaper or online. Then write three questions and answers about the information it represents.

Student _____ Class _____ Date _____

1. The graph below shows the value of a car in relation to the time that has passed since it was purchased. Study the graph and then answer the questions.

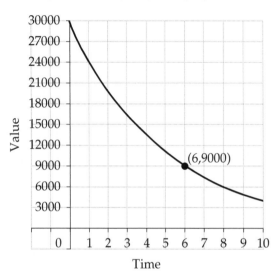

a. This graph shows the relationship between what two quantities?

b. What are the likely units of measurement along the horizontal axis?

c. What are the likely units of measurement along the vertical axis?

d. Is the car increasing or decreasing in value? How can you tell?

e. Is the car's value changing at a constant rate, more and more quickly, or more and more slowly? How can you tell? (You may want to look again at Lesson 1.5 and study the slope triangle.)

f. A point is marked on the curve. Write a sentence about value and time based on the information provided by the coordinates of the point.

g. Estimate the value of the car 1 year after purchase.

h. After approximately how many years will the car be worth $12,000?

i. What information is provided by the y-intercept?

Rising Real Estate Prices

Interpret a quantitative graph of an increasing function with a decreasing rate of change.

Overview

Class Time: 15 minutes

Prerequisites: Students should have completed Lessons 1.1 through 1.5.

In this lesson, students get more practice interpreting graphs—this time, with an increasing function that has a decreasing rate of change. Once again, the function describes the relationship between value and time in years.

Teaching the Lesson

If students made any common omissions or errors on the homework for Lesson 2.3, discuss them before assigning the homework for this lesson.

Homework and Assessment

After finishing the recording sheet, ask students to solve this problem: Look again at the graph in the recording sheet. Write a paragraph describing the relationship between the value of the home and the years since it was purchased. Include details that were not included in the questions on the recording sheet. In particular, choose two points on the curve and write sentences about the information they provide. Also describe the overall trend or pattern in the house's value, in addition to its value at particular moments in time.

Answers to Lesson 2.4 Student Recording Sheet and Homework

STUDENT RECORDING SHEET

1.
   a. The graph shows the relationship between time and value.
   b. The units of measurement along the horizontal axis are likely years. (When introducing this lesson, talk about tracking the value of a house over years. Otherwise, some students may think the appropriate units of measurement are days, hours, or minutes. Also mention that the value of a house or other piece of property usually increases over time.)
   c. The units of measurement along the horizontal axis are likely dollars. (Often, students answer "Money." Try to get them to recognize that money is measured in units, such as dollars.)

d. The value of the house when it was purchased was $160,000.

e. The house's value is increasing. (A typical student answer is "It is going up." Encourage students to write a more complete answer: "As time passes, the value of the house is increasing" or "As we move from left to right along the x-axis, the curve is rising, which shows an increase in the house's value.")

f. The house's value is changing at a slower and slower rate. (Encourage students to see that as time passes, the value increases more and more slowly. Moving from left to right along the x-axis, equal intervals of time correspond with smaller and smaller increases in value.)

g. After six years, the value of the house is $174,000. (Discuss the information provided by several other points if students have a hard time answering this question.)

h. Eight years after purchase, the house will be worth $176,000.

i. The house will be worth $170,000 after approximately three and a half years. (Encourage students to write complete sentences with reference to time and value. They tend to provide only numbers.)

HOMEWORK

Answers will vary. The point (1,164000) corresponds to the sentence, "After one year the house was worth $164000" while the point (4,171000) gives us the information that after four years the house was worth $171,000. Notice that the rate of increase after one year is about twice as big as the rate after four years. The slope of the curve at 1 is twice the slope at 4.

Extend the Learning: Find a graph about two real-world quantities in a newspaper or online. Then write three questions and answers about the information it represents.

Student _____ Class _____ Date _____

1. The graph below shows the value of a house in relation to the time that has passed since its purchase. Study the graph and then answer the questions.

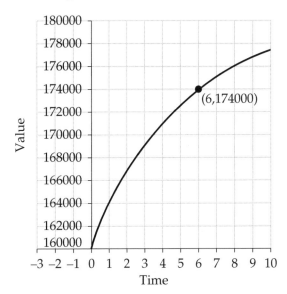

a. This graph shows the relationship between what two quantities?

b. What are the likely units of measurement along the horizontal axis?

c. What are the likely units of measurement along the vertical axis?

d. What was the value of the house when it was purchased?

e. Is the house increasing or decreasing in value? How can you tell?

f. Is the house's value changing at a constant rate, more and more quickly, or more and more slowly? How can you tell?

g. A point is marked on the curve. Write a sentence about value and time based on the information provided by the coordinates of the point.

h. Estimate the value of the house 8 years after purchase.

i. After approximately how much time will the house be worth $170,000?

Perimeter of a Square

Use the graph of the linear function y = 4x.

Overview

Class Time: 20 minutes

Prerequisites: Students should be able to read a graph and identify points on a graph. Students should also understand the nature of a square and know how to determine its perimeter using side length.

In this lesson, students explore the relationship between the perimeter of a square and its side length. It looks at a correspondence where the independent variable is not time. The correspondence between side length (the independent variable) and perimeter (the dependent variable) is linear.

Teaching the Lesson

In this lesson, perimeter is considered as a function of side length. For each side length chosen, a unique perimeter is determined. The quantity that is input into a relationship (side length here) is called the *independent variable* and the quantity that emerges (perimeter in this case) is called the *dependent variable*. Each time the side length is increased by 1 unit the perimeter increases by 4 units. This shows a constant rate of change and the function is called *linear*. Start the lesson by drawing squares, indicating a side length and asking about the perimeter. If a more complicated exercise seems appropriate, you can indicate a perimeter and ask about the side length, or give students half a side length and then ask for the perimeter. Make sure all the students are comfortable with the relationship and can easily move from side length to perimeter. The relationship Perimeter = 4 × Side Length can be written down on the board and symbolized. If we let x stand for side length and y for perimeter, we get $y = 4x$.

Homework and Assessment

For homework after finishing the recording sheet, ask students to solve this problem:

1. A rectangle has a fixed width of 3 inches on each side:

   3 [   ] 3

The graph below shows how the perimeter of the rectangle relates to its bottom length.

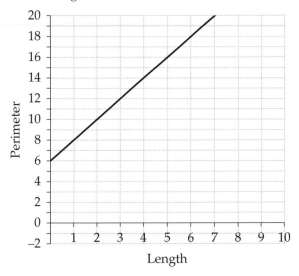

Length

a. Using the information provided in the graph, write three sentences about the perimeter given various bottom lengths—for example, "If the bottom length is 2 inches, then the perimeter of the rectangle is 10 inches."

b. Explain why the curve is shaped the way it is. To do so, think about this question: If you were given a bottom length and asked to find the perimeter of a rectangle without using the graph, how would you do it?

Answers to Lesson 2.5 Student Recording Sheet and Homework

STUDENT RECORDING SHEET

1.
a. The graph shows the relationship between the perimeter and the side length of a square.

b. The units along the horizontal axis are units used to measure length. Likely units of measurement include inches, feet, centimeters, and meters.

c. The units of measurement along the vertical axis must be the same as those for the horizontal axis.

d. As the side length increases, the perimeter of the square increases. As you move from left to right along the x-axis, the curve rises.

e. The perimeter of the square is changing at a constant rate. Each unit increase in side length results in the same increase in perimeter. When the side length changes by 1 unit, the perimeter changes by 4 units.

f. If the side length is 12 inches, then the perimeter is 48 inches.

g. If the side length is 6 inches, then the perimeter is 24 inches.

h. If the perimeter is 20 inches, then the side length is 5 inches.

i.

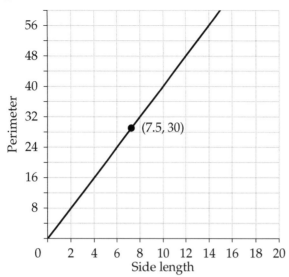

2. The formula for determining the perimeter (P) of a square based on its side length (s) is $P = 4s$. All of the points on the curve reflect the formula—for example, (1,4), (2,8), (3,12), and so on.

HOMEWORK

1.

   a. Answers will vary. Some possibilities include the following:
- If the bottom length is 3 inches, then the perimeter of the rectangle is 12 inches.
- If the bottom length is 4 inches, then the perimeter of the rectangle is 14 inches.

   b. Since the sides are fixed at 3 inches, for any chosen bottom length, the perimeter will be two times that length plus 6 (the length of the two fixed sides).

> **Extend the Learning:** Determine the perimeter of your classroom, or estimate the perimeter of your school building.

Perimeter of a Square
Student Recording Sheet

1. The graph below shows how the perimeter of a square relates to its side length.

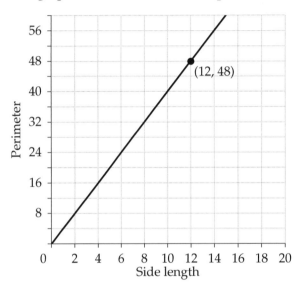

a. This graph shows the relationship between which two quantities?

b. What are the likely units of measurement along the horizontal axis?

c. Based on your answer to Question b, what must be the units of measurement along the vertical axis?

d. As the side length increases, does the perimeter of the square increase or decrease? How can you tell? (Answer this and the following questions using complete sentences.)

(continued)

From *It's All Connected: The Power of Representation to Build Algebraic Reasoning, Grades 6–9* by Frances Van Dyke. © 2012 by Scholastic Inc. Permission granted to photocopy for nonprofit use in a classroom or similar place dedicated to face-to-face educational purposes. Downloadable at www.mathsolutions.com/itsallconnectedalgebrareproducibles.

e. Is the perimeter of the square changing at a constant rate, more and more quickly, or more and more slowly? How can you tell?

f. A point is marked on the curve. Write a sentence about the square's perimeter and side length using the information provided by the coordinates of the point.

g. What is the perimeter when the side length is 6?

h. What is the side length when the perimeter is 20?

i. If the side length is 7.5, then the perimeter is 30. Mark the point on the curve that provides this information.

2. Create a formula for determining the perimeter of a square based on its side length. Test the accuracy of your formula using some of the points on the curve.

Area of a Square

Use the graph of the quadratic function $y = x^2$.

Overview

Class Time: 20 minutes

Prerequisites: Students should have completed Lessons 1.1 through 1.5, and 2.5. Students should also understand the nature of a square and know how to determine its area using side length.

In this lesson, students explore the relationship between the side length and the area of a square. This time, the rate of change is not constant as side length increases.

Teaching the Lesson

As in Lesson 2.4, draw squares and ask about the area for different side lengths. If you feel a more challenging exercise is appropriate, give areas and ask for side lengths, and/or give half size lengths and ask about the area. Once again, ask the standard questions about graphs: "Given x, what is y?" and "Given y, what is x?"

Homework and Assessment

For homework after finishing the recording sheet, ask students to solve this problem:

1. A rectangle has sides 2 inches longer than its top and bottom:

The following graph shows how the area of the rectangle relates to its bottom length.

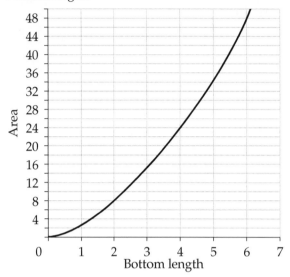

a. Using the information provided in the graph, write three sentences about the area given various bottom lengths—for example, "If the bottom length is 4 inches, then the area of the rectangle is 24 square inches."

b. Explain why the curve is shaped the way it is. To do so, think about this question: If you were given a bottom length and asked to find the area of a square without using the graph, how would you do it?

Answers to Lesson 2.6 Student Recording Sheet and Homework

STUDENT RECORDING SHEET

1.
   a. The graph shows the relationship between the area and the side length of a square.
   b. The units along the horizontal axis are used to measure length. Likely units of measurement include inches, feet, centimeters, and meters.
   c. The units of measurement along the vertical axis must be the square of those used along the horizontal axis.
   d. As the side length increases, the area of the square increases. As you move from left to right along the x-axis, the curve rises.
   e. The area of the square is changing more and more quickly. Each unit increase in side length results in a greater increase in area.
   f. If the side length is 5 inches, then the area is 25 square inches.
   g. If the side length is 7 inches, then the area is 49 square inches.
   h. If the area is 64 square inches, then the side length is 8 inches.

i.

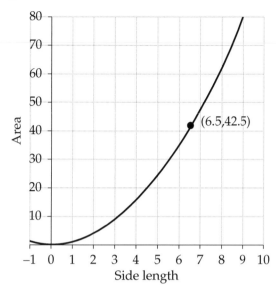

Side length

2. The formula for determining the area of a square based on its side length is Area = Side Length squared, or $y = x^2$. All of the points on the curve reflect the formula—for example, (2,4), (3,9), (4,16), and so on.

HOMEWORK

1.
   a. Answers will vary. Some possibilities include the following:
      - If the bottom length is 2 inches, then the area of the rectangle is 8 square inches.
      - If the bottom length is 6 inches, then the area of the rectangle is 48 square inches.
   b. Since the sides are 2 inches longer than the bottom length, the area will be that length times two more than that length. Symbolically $y = x(x + 2)$, as area = length(length + 2).

> **Extend the Learning:**
> Determine the area of your classroom, or estimate the area of your school building.

1. The graph below shows how the area of a square relates to its side length.

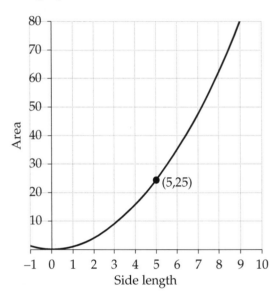

a. This graph shows the relationship between which two quantities?

b. What are the likely units of measurement along the horizontal axis?

c. Based on your answer to Question b, what must be the units of measurement along the vertical axis?

d. As the side length increases, does the area of the square increase or decrease? How can you tell? (Answer this and the following questions using complete sentences.)

(continued)

e. Is the area of the square changing at a constant rate, more and more quickly, or more and more slowly? How can you tell?

f. A point is marked on the curve. Write a sentence about square's area and side length using the information provided by the coordinates of the point.

g. What is the area when the side length is 7 units?

h. What is the side length when the area is 64 square units?

i. If the side length is 6.5 units, then the area is 42.25 square units. Mark the point on the curve that provides this information.

2. Create a formula for determining the area of a square based on the side length. Test the accuracy of your formula using some of the points on the curve.

A Rumor in the Classroom

Interpret a graph with a point of inflection.

Overview

Class Time: 15 minutes

Prerequisites: Students should have completed Lessons 1.1 through 1.4 and 2.1.

In this lesson, students are introduced to the concept of a point of inflection.

Teaching the Lesson

In this lesson students are introduced to the concept of a point of inflection. In addition, they again identify the units of measurement, locate values, and translate points into statements based on the application.

Homework and Assessment

For homework after finishing the recording sheet, ask students to solve these problems:

1. Suppose a class has thirty people in it, and three people start a rumor. What would that graph look like? Compare and contrast this graph with the one shown on the recording sheet.
2. A company president claimed at first that the company's debt was increasing at an increasing rate but now claims the debt is increasing at a decreasing rate. What would that graph look like compared to the graph on the recording sheet?

Answers to Lesson 2.7 Student Recording Sheet and Homework

STUDENT RECORDING SHEET

1.
   a. The graph shows the relationship between time and people who have heard the rumor.
   b. The units of measurement along the *x*-axis are minutes.
   c. The units of measurement along the *y*-axis are numbers of people.
   d. Two people start the rumor.

e. There are twenty-four people in the class. (Recall that the introduction to the problem says that everyone has heard the rumor within ten minutes.)

f. The function is increasing for the first 7 minutes and then remains constant. This is shown by the curve's rising and then remaining at the same level as we move along the x-axis from left to right. (A typical student answer to this question is "It goes up." Encourage students to write a more complete answer, such as, "As time passes, the y value is going up and then remaining at the same level" or "As we move from left to right along the x-axis, the curve is rising and then remaining at the same level.")

g. The point of inflection is at about (2.5,12).

h. At the point of inflection, twelve people have heard the rumor.

i. At the point of inflection, it has been about two and a half minutes since the rumor started.

j. After four and a half minutes, twenty-two people have heard the rumor.

k. The y-intercept is the number of people who first heard the rumor.

HOMEWORK

1. The graph would have a y-intercept of 3, not 2. It would level off at 30, not 24.

2. The graph showing the company's debt over time will also look like the graph on the recording sheet.

Extend the Learning: The population of a species of animals on an island often has the shape of the "rumor" graph. Can you explain why? Suppose the population starts with twenty-five animals and levels off at 300 after six years. Assume the point of inflection is at (2,150). Draw the graph, and use it as the basis for your explanation.

Student _____ Class _____ Date _____

A Rumor in the Classroom
Student Recording Sheet

1. A rumor is spreading quickly among the students in a classroom, and within ten minutes, everyone has heard it. The graph below shows the number of people who have heard the rumor in relation to the time that has passed since the rumor was started.

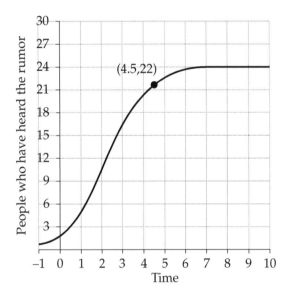

a. This graph shows the relationship between what two quantities?

b. What are the units of measurement along the *x*-axis?

c. What are the units of measurement along the *y*-axis?

d. How many people start the rumor?

(continued)

e. How many people are in the class?

f. The relationship between the quantities on this graph is called a *function*, because each *x* value leads to one and only one *y* value. Is the function decreasing? How can you tell?

g. The function changes more and more quickly and then more and more slowly. The point at which it shifts from faster and faster to slower and slower is called the *point of inflection*. Find and mark the point of inflection on the curve.

h. At the point of inflection, how many people have heard the rumor?

i. At the point of inflection, how long has it been since the rumor started?

j. A point is marked on the curve. Write a sentence about the rumor based on the information provided by the coordinates of the point.

k. What does the *y*-intercept mean in terms of this problem?

Using a Motion Detector

Interpret a quantitative graph of a decreasing function with a decreasing rate of change.

Overview

Class Time: 15 minutes

Prerequisites: Students should have completed Lessons 1.1 through 1.3, 1.7, and Lessons 2.1 through 2.3.

In this lesson, students may have the opportunity to create a graph themselves using a motion detector. If one is not available, they revisit the application of distance from an object in terms of time, first seen in Lessons 1.7, 1.10, and 1.11.

Teaching the Lesson

This exercise can be done with or without a motion detector. If you have access to one, demonstrate its use to students. In the lesson, a person walks toward and away from a motion detector while it records his distance from it for a period of 15 seconds. Students should look at the graph of this information both locally and globally. Then they should answer the standard questions—"Given x, what is y?" and "Given y, what is x?"—and interpret the rate of change.

Homework and Assessment

For homework after finishing the recording sheet, ask students to solve this problem: Draw a graph of a person walking in front of a motion detector. Also write three questions about the graph and provide the answers.

STUDENT RECORDING SHEET

1.
   a. The graph shows the relationship between time and distance.
   b. The units of measurement along the horizontal axis are seconds.
   c. The units of measurement along the vertical axis are feet.
   d. Mr. Feucht is walking toward the motion detector. As time passes, his distance from it decreases. (A typical student answer is "It goes down." Encourage students to write a more complete answer, such as "As time passes, the distance decreases" or "As we move from left to right along the *x*-axis, the curve is falling.")
   e. Mr. Feucht is moving more and more quickly. (Students have a hard time explaining why this is so, and most will not try. Encourage students to see that as time passes, Mr. Feucht's distance from the motion detector decreases at a faster and faster rate. As we move from left to right along the *x*-axis, equal intervals of time are associated with bigger and bigger decreases in distance.)
   f. At the beginning of the time period, Mr. Feucht is fourteen feet away. This point is the *y*-intercept, and it corresponds to his distance from the detector when he starts walking.
   g. After eight seconds, Mr. Feucht is ten feet away from the motion detector.
   h. The point marked on the curve should be directly above the 6 on the horizontal axis.
   i. Mr. Feucht walks for thirteen and a half seconds before reaching the motion detector.
   j. After two seconds, Mr. Feucht is thirteen and a half feet from the detector.
   k. Mr. Feucht is four feet from the motion detector after twelve seconds. (Students tend to answer these questions with only numbers. Encourage them to write complete sentences that refer to both time and distance. Model a sample response before assigning this recording sheet.)
2. The *y*-intercept represents Mr. Feucht's original distance from the motion detector.

HOMEWORK

Answers will vary.

Extend the Learning: Consider the following graph; it records Cecilia's distance in feet from the motion detector in terms of time in seconds, when she walked in front of it. Write a paragraph about her walk, giving as many details as you can.

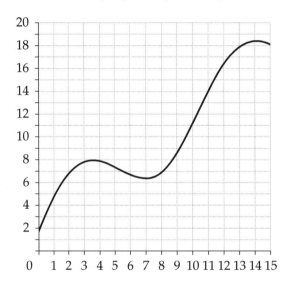

Possible Answer: She starts off 2 feet away and for the first 3.5 seconds backs away until she is 8 feet away. She slowly moves toward it and after 7 seconds is about 6.3 feet away. She then moves away from the detector and after 14 seconds is 18.5 feet away.

In the final second she starts back toward the detector.

A very observant student may look at the time interval from 11 to 12, and note her speed is about 3 feet per second at that moment. This is at the point of inflection where the graph is the steepest and thus her speed is the greatest.

Using a Motion Detector

Student Recording Sheet

1. Mr. Feucht walked in front of a motion detector, and the information is recorded on the graph below.

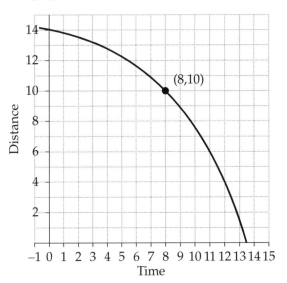

a. This graph shows the relationship between what two quantities?

b. What are the units of measurement along the horizontal axis?

c. What are the units of measurement along the vertical axis?

d. Is Mr. Feucht walking toward the motion detector or away from it? How can you tell?

(continued)

From *It's All Connected: The Power of Representation to Build Algebraic Reasoning, Grades 6–9* by Frances Van Dyke. © 2012 by Scholastic Inc. Permission granted to photocopy for nonprofit use in a classroom or similar place dedicated to face-to-face educational purposes. Downloadable at www.mathsolutions.com/itsallconnectedalgebrareproducibles.

e. Is Mr. Feucht moving at a constant rate, more and more quickly, or more and more slowly? How can you tell?

f. At the beginning of the time period, how far away from the motion detector is Mr. Feucht?

g. A point is marked on the curve. Write a sentence about Mr. Feucht's distance from the motion detector using the information provided by the coordinates of the point.

h. After six seconds, Mr. Feucht is about eleven and a half feet from the motion detector. Mark the point on the curve that provides this information.

i. For how long does Mr. Feucht walk before he reaches the motion detector?

j. How far away from the motion detector is Mr. Feucht after two seconds?

k. Mr. Feucht is four feet from the motion detector after how many seconds?

2. What does the y-intercept represent in this problem?

2.9

Mark's Distance from the Cafeteria

Work with a distance-versus-time graph.

Overview

Class Time: 15 minutes

Prerequisites: Students should have completed Lessons 1.1 through 1.5 and Lessons 2.1 through 2.3.

Similar to Lesson 2.7, this lesson requires students to look at a graph in its entirety, as well as at specific points. Students need to see that a curve that is concave up specifies an increasing rate of change.

Teaching the Lesson

In completing the recording sheet, students must determine the scale along each axis. They can determine the values of the tick marks using the point that is marked on the curve.

Homework and Assessment

HOMEWORK

For homework after finishing the recording sheet, ask students to solve this problem: Draw a distance-versus-time graph that represents a person walking away from school. Mark a point on the curve, and write a corresponding sentence. Determine the scale on each axis, based on your point. What are the values of the tick marks on each axis?

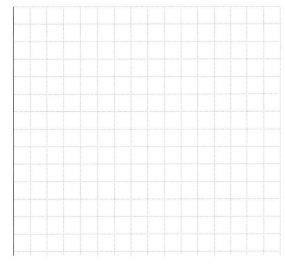

STUDENT RECORDING SHEET

1.
   a. The graph shows the relationship between time and distance.
   b. The likely units of measurement along the horizontal axis are seconds.
   c. The likely units of measurement along the vertical axis are feet or yards.
   d. Mark is walking away from the cafeteria. As time passes, his distance from the cafeteria increases. (A typical student answer is "It goes up." Encourage students to write a more complete answer, such as "As time passes, the distance increases" or "As we move from left to right along the horizontal axis, the curve is rising.")
   e. Mark is speeding up as he walks. As time passes, the distance increases more and more quickly. (Students often have a hard time explaining this, and most will not try. Encourage them to see that as time passes, Mark's distance from the cafeteria increases as each second passes. Moving from left to right along the *x*-axis, equal intervals of time correspond with bigger and bigger increases in distance.)
   f. After 14 seconds, Mark is 12 feet (or yards) from the cafeteria.
   g. Along the *x*-axis, where the units of measurement are seconds, the values of the tick marks are 2, 4, 6, 8, and so on. Along the *y*-axis, where the units of measurement are feet or yards, the values of the tick marks are 3, 6, 9, 12, and so on. (If students have a hard time with this, determine the scale using another point on the curve.)
   h. After 18 seconds, Mark is 18 feet or yards away from the cafeteria.
   i. Mark begins 3 feet or yards away from the cafeteria.
   j. Mark is 9 feet from the cafeteria after 11 seconds. (Encourage students to write full sentences with reference to time and distance. They tend to put down just numbers.)

HOMEWORK

Make sure students can justify their choice of scale and explain their vision of the motion.

Answers will vary. One possibility might be: Frederica lives one mile from school and it takes her around twenty minutes to get home. The units along the *x*-axis represent minutes and a single unit in line with the top of the graph can represent one mile. She walked home from school, got to her house, and realized she did not have her Math book so went back to school to get it. It took her twenty-two minutes to walk the mile.

Extend the Learning: Consider the graph below; it represents Frederica's distance from school in terms of time. Make up a story to go with the graph including as many details from the graph as possible. Be sure to indicate your choice of units of measurement. Along the axes and choose a scale for the y-axis.

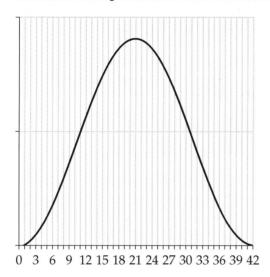

0 3 6 9 12 15 18 21 24 27 30 33 36 39 42

Student _____ Class _____ Date _____

LESSON **2.9** **Mark's Distance from the Cafeteria**
Student Recording Sheet

1. Consider the graph below. It portrays Mark's distance from the cafeteria in relation to the time elapsed since the bell rang. Study the graph and answer the questions.

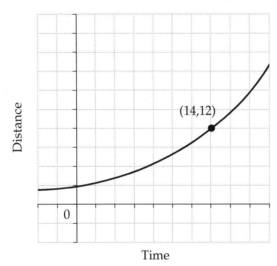

a. This graph shows the relationship between what two quantities?

b. What are the likely units of measurement along the horizontal axis?

c. What are the likely units of measurement along the vertical axis?

d. Is Mark walking away from the cafeteria or toward the cafeteria? How can you tell?

(continued)

e. Is Mark speeding up as he walks or slowing down? How can you tell?

f. A point is marked on the curve. Write a sentence about distance and time using the information provided by the coordinates of the point.

g. Use the coordinates of the point to help you fill in the scale along each axis. What are the values of the tick marks?

h. Estimate how far from the cafeteria Mark is after eighteen seconds.

i. How far from the cafeteria does Mark begin?

j. After how long is Mark nine feet from the cafeteria?

Value of a Boat

Work with a decreasing function with an increasing rate of change.

Overview

Class Time: 20 minutes

Prerequisites: Students should have completed Lessons 1.1 through 1.5, plus Lessons 2.1 and 2.6.

This lesson is similar to Lesson 2.7, although here, the function is decreasing. Students once again work with the relationship of value in terms of time.

Teaching the Lesson

To correctly answer the first four on the recording sheet, students must incorporate the concepts from Section I. The identified point and questions about the scale/tick marks require understanding the mechanics of quantitative graphs.

Homework and Assessment

For homework after finishing the recording sheet, ask students to solve this problem (which is similar to the homework problems in Lessons 2.8 and 2.9):

1. Sally is walking. The graph below represents her distance from the beach in terms of time.

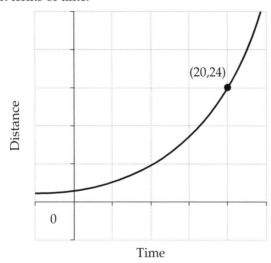

a. Is Sally walking toward the beach or away from the beach? How do you know?
b. Does Sally walk at a steady pace, faster and faster, or slower and slower? How do you know?
c. What are the likely units of measurement along the *x*-axis?
d. What are the likely units of measurement along the *y*-axis?
e. A point is marked on the graph. Write a sentence about the situation based on the information provided by this point.
f. Tick marks are shown along the *x*-axis. Use the point to help you determine the scale and find the values of these tick marks.
g. Tick marks are shown along the *y*-axis. Use the point to help you determine the scale and find the values of these tick marks.
h. How far from the beach does Sally start?
i. How far is Sally from the beach after ten seconds?
j. When is Sally forty feet from the beach?

Answers to Lesson 2.10 Student Recording Sheet and Homework

STUDENT RECORDING SHEET

1.
   a. The graph shows the relationship between time and value.
   b. The likely units of measurement along the horizontal axis are years. (When introducing this lesson to students, talk about tracking the value of things over years. Otherwise, some students may think appropriate answers to the question include days, hours, and minutes.)
   c. The likely units of measurement along the vertical axis are dollars. (Often, students answer "Money." Encourage them to think about measuring money in terms of units, such as dollars.)
   d. The boat is decreasing in value. (A typical student answer is "It goes down." Encourage students to write a more complete answer, such as "As time passes, the value of the boat is going down" or "As we move from left to right along the *x*-axis, the curve is falling, which means the boat's value is decreasing.")
   e. The boat's value is changing at a slower and slower rate. (Students have a hard time explaining this, and most will not try. Encourage them to see that as time passes, the value decreases more and more slowly. Moving from left to right along the *x*-axis, equal intervals of time correspond to smaller and smaller decreases in value.)
   f. After four years, the value of the boat is $15,000.
   g. Along the *x*-axis, where the units of measurement are years, the values of the tick marks are 2, 4, 6, 8, and so on. Along the *y*-axis, where the units of measurement are dollars, the values of the tick marks are 3,000, 6,000, 9,000, 12,000, and so on. (If students have a hard time with this problem, do other points on the curve.)
   h. The *y*-intercept is $24,000. It represents the original value of the boat.
   i. After 6 years, the boat is worth $12,000.

j. The boat is worth $6,000 after twelve years. (Encourage students to write full sentences in discussing time and value. They tend to put down only numbers.)

k. After five years, the boat is worth about $13,500.

HOMEWORK

1.
a. Sally is walking away from the beach. Distance increases as time passes.
b. Sally is walking faster and faster. As time passes, equal intervals of time correspond to more and more distance being covered.
c. The units of measurement along the x-axis are likely seconds.
d. The units of measurement along the y-axis are likely feet.
e. After twenty seconds, Sally is twenty-four feet away from the beach.
f. The values of tick marks along the x-axis are 5, 10, 15, 20, and 25 (seconds).
g. The values of the tick marks along the y-axis are 8, 16, 24, 32, and 40 (feet).
h. Sally starts about two feet from the beach. (Point out that the y-intercept is about one-quarter of the way to the first tick mark, which has a value of 8.)
i. After ten seconds, Sally is about eight feet from the beach.
j. Sally is forty feet from the beach after about twenty-five seconds.

Extend the Learning: Make up a problem of this type for the class. Create a graph that includes a marked point and tick marks along the axes. Ask three questions about the graph, and provide the answers.

Student _____ Class _____ Date _____

Value of a Boat
Student Recording Sheet

1. Look at the graph below. It represents the value of a boat in relation to the time since it was purchased. Study the graph and answer the questions.

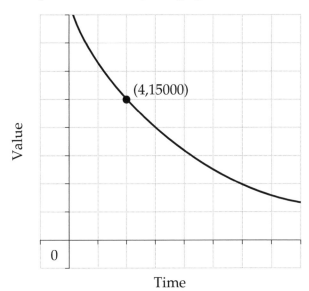

(4,15000)

Value

Time

0

a. This graph shows the relationship between which two quantities?

b. What are the likely units of measurement along the horizontal axis?

c. What are the likely units of measurement along the vertical axis?

d. Is the boat increasing or decreasing in value? How can you tell?

(continued)

e. Is the boat's value changing at a constant rate, faster and faster, or slower and slower? How can you tell?

f. A point is marked on the curve. Write a sentence about value and time using the information provided by the coordinates of the point.

g. Fill in the scale along each axis, using the coordinates of the point to help you. What are the values of the tick marks? (You will likely find it easy to determine the values of the tick marks along the horizontal axis, but be careful determining the tick marks along the vertical axis.

h. What is the y-intercept, and what is its significance in terms of the boat's value?

i. How much is the boat worth after six years?

j. When is the boat worth $6,000?

k. How much is the boat worth after five years?

l. When is the boat worth $21,000?

Rocket in the Air

Work with a quadratic function that models the height of a rocket in terms of time.

Overview

MATH MATTERS

Parabola

A conic section is a curve obtained by intersecting a plane with a cone. These were first studied as far back as 200 BC. A parabola is one such intersection. Its shape is shown on the graph.

Class Time: 25 minutes

Prerequisites: Students should have completed Lessons 2.3 and 2.4.

This lesson introduces students to an application they will see many times throughout high school and college, that of an object thrown up into the air. Its height is graphed in terms of time and the resulting curve is a parabola.

Teaching the Lesson

When an object is shot into the air with an initial velocity of v_0 feet per second from a height of h_0 feet above the ground, the equation $h(t) = -16t^2 + v_0 t + h_0$ is used to model the height of the object $h(t)$ in terms of the time since firing t. In this exercise, $-16t^2 + 180t + 80$ is used. The function is quadratic, and the curve is a parabola facing down. In this lesson, the standard questions of "Given x, what is y?" and "Given y, what is x?" appear as "After x seconds, what is the height of the rocket?" and "When is the rocket y feet above the ground?"

Homework and Assessment

For homework after finishing the recording sheet, ask students to write three more questions and answers about the rocket.

Answers to Lesson 2.11 Student Recording Sheet and Homework

STUDENT RECORDING SHEET

1.
   a. The units of measurement along the x-axis are seconds, and the units of measurement along the y-axis are feet.
   b. After three seconds, the rocket is 420 feet in the air.
   c. The rocket goes up 480 feet.
   d. The initial height of the rocket is a little less than ninety feet.
   e. The rocket is in the air for about ten and a half seconds.
   f. Yes. The rocket is 330 feet in the air after about two seconds and after about eight seconds.

g. Yes. The rocket is thirty feet in the air at just under ten and a half seconds.

h. The rocket is 330 feet in the air on its way up and then again on its way down. Since it is shot off from a platform about ninety feet above the ground, it is at thirty feet only on its way down.

HOMEWORK

Answers will vary. Make sure if a point is chosen and interpreted in terms of height and time that the coordinates do lie on the graph. A possible answer might be that the rocket slows on the way up and gathers speed on the way down.

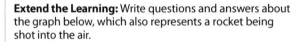

Extend the Learning: Write questions and answers about the graph below, which also represents a rocket being shot into the air.

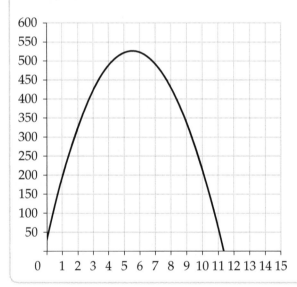

1. When an object is shot up into the air, its height above the ground is a function of time. The graph below represents a rocket shot off from a platform above the ground. The rocket's height is given as a function of time. Study the graph and answer the questions. Be sure to give full answers to the questions. You will need to estimate some of the values.

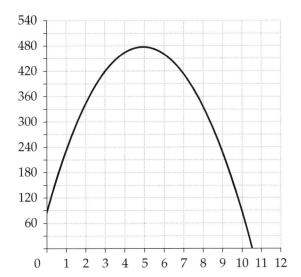

   a. What are the units of measurement along each axis?

   b. How high is the rocket after three seconds?

   c. How high does the rocket go?

   d. What is the initial height of the rocket?

   e. For how long is the rocket in the air?

   f. Is the rocket ever 330 feet in the air? If so, when?

   g. Is the rocket ever thirty feet in the air? If so, when?

   h. Explain why there are two answers to Question f but only one to Question g.

Beehive Rocket

Draw the path of a rocket.

Overview

Class Time: 15 minutes

Prerequisites: Students should have completed Lessons 2.3, 2.4, and 2.11.

In this lesson, students work with the same "rocket" application as in Lesson 2.11, but here, they must draw a graph given the pertinent information.

Teaching the Lesson

Start by asking for observations about the graph in Lesson 2.11. If possible, place it on a transparency on an overhead projector. Ask how would it be different if the rocket reached a maximum height of 700 feet? What would it look like if it was in the air for twenty seconds? This should help students draw the proper graph.

Homework and Assessment

For homework after finishing the recording sheet, ask students to complete this problem:

> A beehive rocket is fired from a stand thirty-five feet high. It stays in the air for seven seconds, and it reaches its maximum height of seventy-five feet after three seconds.

Draw a graph of the relationship between height and time. Label both axes, and assign values to the tick marks to show the scale.

STUDENT RECORDING SHEET

The graph below contains the information required by the problem:

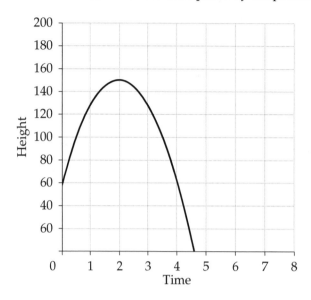

To complete this problem, students need to understand that the *x*-intercept is 4.5 and the *y*-intercept is 60. The tick marks along the *x*-axis could represent intervals of one second, and those along the *y*-axis could represent intervals of twenty feet. Given these scales, the maximum coordinates of (2,150) are visible on the graph.

HOMEWORK

The graph below contains the information required by the problem:

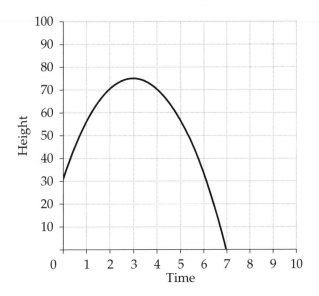

To complete this problem, students need to understand that the *x*-intercept is 7 and the *y*-intercept is 35. The tick marks along the horizontal axis could represent intervals of one second, and those along the *y*-axis could represent intervals of ten feet. Given these scales, the maximum coordinates of (3,75) are visible on the graph.

Extend the Learning: Create a similar "rocket" problem. For the answer, provide a graph and a written description of it.

Student _____ Class _____ Date _____

Beehive Rocket

Student Recording Sheet

A beehive rocket is shot off a platform sixty feet above the ground. It stays in the air for four and a half seconds, and it reaches its maximum height of 150 feet after two seconds. Draw a graph of the relationship between height and time. Label both axes, and provide the values of the tick marks to show the scale.

Including Tables with Graphs

Overview

In this section, the lessons introduce tables to accompany the graphs. This concept will be very familiar to students, because tables are included in the curriculum throughout elementary school. Hopefully, completing Sections I and II will have familiarized students with graphs to the point that they are equally comfortable with graphs as with tables and view the two as equivalent means of representing functions. Achieving this level of familiarity is important to students' later learning. Regrettably, many students enter college having little experience with graphs and thus are reluctant to use them.

In Section III, the applications in the lessons include spread of a virus, distance versus time, value of an object, and height of a projectile. These are all functions students will see in the high school curriculum. The questions asked in earlier lessons about how the functions change are asked in these lessons, as well.

Lessons

LESSON 3.1   **Spread of a Virus**   *110*
Lesson similar to Section II, table introduced at the end.

LESSON 3.2   **Distance from a Dock**   *114*
Table and graph for a constant function.

LESSON 3.3   **Distance from a Motion Detector**   *117*
Given a table, answer questions, and produce a graph.

LESSON 3.4   **Value of an Antique**   *120*
Given a table, consider rate of change and graph.

LESSON 3.5   **Value of a Motorcycle**   *124*
Given a linear relationship, produce a table and a graph.

LESSON 3.6   **Distance from a House**   *129*
Given a graph, choose a table; given a table, choose a sentence.

LESSON 3.7   **Height of a Projectile**   *133*
Given a quadratic function, answer questions, and produce a table.

LESSON 3.8   **Throwing a Grapefruit!**   *137*
Further work with quadratic functions.

FURTHER PRACTICE 3.A   **Your Choice**   *141*
Create your own example.

Spread of a Virus

Lesson similar to Section II, table introduced at the end.

Overview

Class Time: 20 minutes

Prerequisites: Students should have completed Lessons 1.1 through 1.4, 2.1 through 2.4, and 2.7.

In this lesson, students create a table given points on a graph. Our hope is for students to see that functions can be represented as graphs or tables and to develop facility in moving from one to the other in either direction.

Teaching the Lesson

This kind of curve, which was first seen in Lesson 2.7, is a called a *logistic curve*. It is used to model growth that seems exponential at first but then slows down as the rate of increase levels off. Recall that the point where the rate of change stops increasing and starts decreasing is called the *point of inflection*.

An exponential curve represents a function that grows or decays in proportion to the amount present. Its graph then has the shape

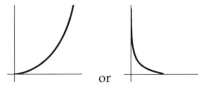

or

Homework and Assessment

For homework after finishing the recording sheet, ask students to solve this problem: In Sections I and II, you learned that a function can be represented by a graph. A function can also be represented by a table, as introduced in this lesson. Each representation—graph and table—has certain advantages over the other. What are the advantages of each? When might it be preferable to have a graph, and when might it be preferable to have a table?

Answers to Lesson 3.1 Student Recording Sheet and Homework

STUDENT RECORDING SHEET

1. Most of this recording sheet is like the one provided in Section II, but the last two questions involve using a table.
   a. The graph shows the relationship between time and people infected by the virus.
   b. The units of measurement along the x-axis are days.
   c. The units of measurement along the y-axis are numbers of people.
   d. Twenty people had the infection to start with.
   e. There are 200 people in the community.
   f. The function is increasing. As we move from left to right along the x-axis, the curve is rising. As time passed, more and more people became infected.
   g. The point of inflection is about (15,115).
2. Here is the completed table, with estimates for the values in the People column:

Days	People
0	20
10	70
20	148
30	185
40	198
50	200

3. Answers will vary. Here is an example: After 40 days, 198 people had become infected with the virus.

HOMEWORK

A graph shows an overall trend. It is continuous and so can show variation easily. A table gives precise values. When trying to see what monthly charge you will need to pay on a mortgage, you would want a table. When trying to compare the effect of paying different rates in different periods of time, you might want a graph.

> **Extend the Learning:** Choose a lesson from Section II, and create a table that corresponds with the graph.

Spread of a Virus
Student Recording Sheet

1. A virus spread throughout a community. Day by day, more and more people became infected until the virus had spread throughout the entire community. The graph below indicates the number of people who became infected as time went by.

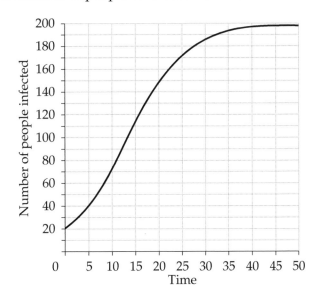

a. This graph shows the relationship between what two quantities?

b. What are the units of measurement along the *x*-axis?

c. What are the units of measurement along the *y*-axis?

d. How many people had the infection to start with?

(continued)

e. How many people are in the community?

f. This relationship is called a *function*, as each *x* value has one and only one *y* value. Is the function increasing or decreasing? How can you tell?

g. The function changes more and more quickly and then more and more slowly. The point at which the rate of change shifts from increasing to decreasing is called a *point of inflection*. Find and mark the point of inflection on the curve.

2. Use the graph to fill in this table:

Days	People
0	
10	
20	
30	
40	
50	

3. Choose one row from the table. Write a sentence about the virus using the information provided in that row.

Distance from a Dock

Table and graph for a constant function.

Overview

Class Time: 15 minutes

Prerequisites: Students should understand the nature of a constant function, first seen in Lesson 1.1.

This lesson introduces students to the table corresponding to a constant function. The table provides precise information about particular *x*-values but cannot provide information about all the *x*-values the way a graph can.

Teaching the Lesson

This lesson presents a table associated with a graph. The function displayed is constant.

From the graph, we can conclude that Ralph stood 25 feet away from the dock for the full 5 minutes. From the table, we can only really conclude that he was exactly 25 feet from the dock at each minute. He could have been somewhere else during the intervening times. Because the graph is continuous, it gives us a more complete picture than the table.

By nature, a table provides discrete data, whereas a graph depicts an overall trend. Because this graph is continuous, every instance in the relationship is accounted for. Of course, in most instances, if the independent variable is time and the data are collected every fraction of a second, the relationship being examined will most likely be accurately portrayed.

When an algebraic function is used to model a situation, the result is a continuous representation, as long as the function itself is continuous. For every input value, the function provides an output value. Of course, the accuracy of the information depends on how good the model is.

Homework and Assessment

For homework after finishing the recording sheet, ask students to solve this problem: If the graph on the recording sheet showed only a black dot at the height of 25 directly above 5, what could you conclude?

STUDENT RECORDING SHEET

1.
   a. The graph of a horizontal line indicates a constant function. As time passes, Ralph's distance from the dock remains constant at 25 feet. In the table, for each value of time, the distance is the same: 25 feet.
   b. There is a continuous horizontal line because Ralph's distance from the dock is 25 feet the entire time. Black dots above the numbers along the x-axis would indicate that Ralph's distance from the dock was 25 feet at only those particular instances.
   c. Answers will vary. Here is an example sentence: At 3 minutes, Ralph was 25 feet from the dock.

2.
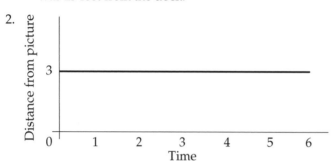

Time (in minutes)	Distance from painting (in feet)
1	3
2	3
3	3
4	3
5	3
6	3

HOMEWORK

A single dot would correspond to the sentence, "After 5 minutes Ralph's distance from the dock was 25 feet." One could not draw any conclusion about where he was at other points in time.

> **Extend the Learning:** Make up a problem of this type, and provide the corresponding graph and table.

Student _____ Class _____ Date _____

Distance from a Dock
Student Recording Sheet

1. Ralph stood 25 feet from the dock for 5 minutes. The graph and the table below represent this situation:

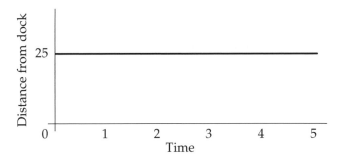

Time (in minutes)	Distance from dock (in feet)
1	25
2	25
3	25
4	25
5	25

   a. Write a few sentences explaining the graph and the table.

   b. On the graph, why is there a continuous horizontal line and not just dots above the numbers along the *x*-axis (1, 2, 3, 4, and 5)?

   c. Choose one row in the table. Write a sentence about Ralph's distance from the dock using the information in that row.

2. Rachida stood 3 feet from a painting for 6 minutes. Draw a graph and produce a table corresponding to this situation.

Distance from a Motion Detector

Given a table, answer questions, and produce a graph.

Overview

Class Time: 15 minutes

Prerequisites: It would be helpful for students to have some experience with a motion detector (see Lesson 2.8).

In this lesson, for the first time, students create a graph from a table. It reinforces the idea that many different graphs can correspond to the same table. Likewise by choosing different x-values, different tables can correspond to the same graph.

Teaching the Lesson

In this lesson, students are given a table, asked several questions about it, and then required to produce a corresponding graph. Once again, because the graph is continuous and the table is discrete, the graph cannot be drawn with real precision. There are an infinite number of possibilities for the times that are not shown.

Homework and Assessment

For homework after finishing the recording sheet, ask students to solve this problem: In the problem on the recording sheet, is it possible that Ashley walked toward the motion detector more than once? Why or why not?

Answers to Lesson 3.3 Student Recording Sheet and Homework

STUDENT RECORDING SHEET

1.
   a. The units of measurement for the first column are seconds.
   b. The units of measurement for the second column are feet.
   c. Answers will vary. Here is one example sentence: After 12 seconds, Ashley was 9 feet from the motion detector.
   d. Ashley was 5 feet from the motion detector at the start.
   e. Ashley seems to have moved away from the motion detector at first, reaching a distance of 12 feet after 4 seconds. It seems she next moves toward the detector, reaching a distance of 6 feet after 10 seconds. It

then appears she moved away again, reaching a distance of 12.5 feet after 14 seconds.

f.

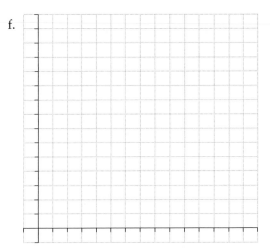

HOMEWORK

Yes, it is possible that Ashley walked toward the motion detector more than once. Not all times are shown—only those at 2-second intervals. For instance, at 5 seconds, Ashley could have been 9 feet away, having moved forward between 4 and 5 seconds.

Extend the Learning: Create a table corresponding to this situation: Jared started 10 feet away from the motion detector. He moved toward it for the first 3 seconds, stopping at 4 feet away. After standing still for 3 seconds, he moved away from the motion detector, reaching 10 feet away after 10 seconds. Is only one table correct for this situation? Why or why not?

From *It's All Connected: The Power of Representation to Build Algebraic Reasoning, Grades 6–9* by Frances Van Dyke. © 2012 by Scholastic Inc. Permission granted to photocopy for nonprofit use in a classroom or similar place dedicated to face-to-face educational purposes. Downloadable at www.mathsolutions.com/itsallconnectedalgebrareproducibles.

LESSON 3.3 Distance from a Motion Detector
Student Recording Sheet

1. The table below shows the relationship between distance and time when Ashley walked in front of a motion detector. A motion detector tracks a person's distance from it in feet for fifteen seconds. Study the table and answer the questions.

Time	Distance
0	5
2	8
4	12
6	10
8	6.5
10	6
12	9
14	2.5

   a. What are the units of measurement for the first column?

   b. What are the units of measurement for the second column?

   c. Choose a row in the table. Write a sentence about Ashley's distance from the motion detector based on the information in that row.

   d. How far was Ashley from the motion detector at the start?

   e. Describe Ashley's movement in terms of her distance from the motion detector over time.

   f. Graph the relationship. Be sure to label the axes and indicate the scales by providing values for the tick marks.

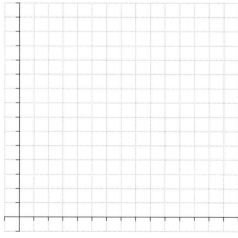

Value of an Antique

Given a table, consider rate of change and graph.

Overview

Class Time: 20 minutes

Prerequisites: Students should have completed Lessons 1.1 through 1.4.

In this lesson, students once again start with a table and answer questions about it in terms of the application. This time, they perform the added step of determining that the value is increasing but at a decreasing rate of change.

Teaching the Lesson

Start by asking students to describe how they can tell from a graph if a function is increasing. (As our eyes move from left to right if the curve is rising, the function is increasing.) Given that a function is increasing, ask them how you decide if the function is increasing at a steady rate, faster and faster or slower and slower. (If the shape is a straight line with positive slope, the function is increasing at a steady rate. If its shape is

it is increasing faster and faster. With the shape

it is increasing slower and slower.

We wish to make the same distinction with a table. Looking at a table, how can we tell if the function is increasing? If it is increasing, how can we tell if the increase is at a steady rate, faster and faster or more and more slowly? What assumptions must we make? We need to assume the values given reflect the general trend. We start with equally spaced increasing x-values. If the y-values are equally spaced and increasing, we figure the function is increasing at a steady rate. If the y-values are increasing and the difference between consecutive pairs is getting larger and larger, it appears the function is increasing faster and faster. If the y-values are increasing but the difference between consecutive pairs is getting smaller and smaller, it appears the function is increasing more and more slowly.

Homework and Assessment

For homework after finishing the recording sheet, ask students to solve this problem: *Describe a table showing the value of an object over time when the value of the object is increasing faster and faster in terms of time. Identify the object and the units of measurement for time.*

Answers to Lesson 3.4 Student Recording Sheet and Handout

STUDENT RECORDING SHEET

1.
   a. The units of measurement for the first column are years.
   b. The units of measurement for the second column are dollars.
   c. Answers will vary. Here is an example sentence: After six years, the antique is worth $645.
   d. The original value of the antique was $200.
   e. As time passes, the value of the antique is increasing.
   f. The value of the antique is changing at a slower and slower rate.
   g. The curve would be shaped like this:

   h. The graph below includes all of the elements required by the problem:

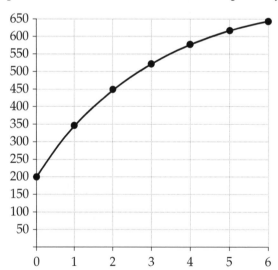

HOMEWORK

In general, the numbers in the second column must be increasing and doing so by larger and larger amounts compared with the constantly increasing numbers in the first column. Students' objects will vary, but the units of measurement for time will likely be years in most cases.

> **Extend the Learning:** In a table representing time versus value, is it possible for the numbers in the right-hand column (Value) to increase faster and faster but for the value of the object not to increase faster and faster? Explain your answer.
>
> **Answer:** If the numbers in the lefthand column (Time) of the table are increasing faster and faster, the increase in value may be at a constant rate or even a rate that is slowing down. In the introduction to the lesson, we note that in order to make the determination we want the numbers that are input to be increasing at a steady rate. Then we can determine how the output numbers are behaving in comparison.

LESSON 3.4 Value of an Antique
Student Recording Sheet

1. The table below shows the relationship between the value of an antique and the time since it was purchased. Study the table and answer the questions.

Time	Value
0	200
1	350
2	450
3	525
4	575
5	620
6	645

a. What are the likely units of measurement for the first column?

b. What are the likely units of measurement for the second column?

c. Choose a row in the table. Write a sentence about the value of the antique over time using the information in that row.

d. What was the original value of the antique?

e. As time passes, is the value of the antique increasing or decreasing?

f. Is the value changing at a constant rate, faster and faster, or slower and slower?

g. If you were to graph the relationship between value and time, which of the following shapes would the curve look like? Circle the correct one.

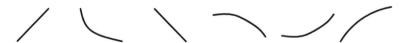

(continued)

h. Graph the relationship. Label each axis and provide the scale, indicating the values of the tick marks.

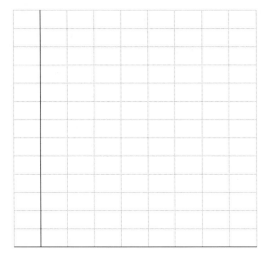

Value of a Motorcycle

Given a linear relationship, produce a table and a graph.

Overview

Class Time: 20 minutes

Prerequisites: Students should be familiar with the the relationship between value and time as addressed in Lessons 1.1 and 2.3.

In this lesson, students create a table with a constant rate of change, answer questions about the table, and then produce a graph using the table information.

Teaching the Lesson

The concept taught in this lesson is that of a linear function, which students will become thoroughly familiar with. Often, difficult functions are estimated by linear approximations over small intervals. In calculus, students find tangent lines to curves, which leads to making linear approximations for functions.

Homework and Assessment

For homework after finishing the recording sheet, ask students to answer these questions:

1. Look at the graph you created on the recording sheet. What if the curve started further up on the *y*-axis? What would that mean about the value of the motorcycle?
2. What if the curve was linear but dropped more steeply? What would that mean about the value of the motorcycle?

In addition, you may want to assign Supplementary Lesson 3.1.

STUDENT RECORDING SHEET

1.

a.

Time	Value
0	28,000
1	25,000
2	22,000
3	19,000
4	16,000
5	13,000
6	10,000
7	7,000
8	4,000

b. The units of measurement for the first column are years.

c. The units of measurement for the second column are dollars.

d. Answers will vary. Here is an example sentence: After three years, the motorcycle was worth $19,000.

e. After seven years, the motorcycle was worth $7,000.

f. The motorcycle was worth $16,000 after four years.

g. The value of the motorcycle is changing at a constant rate.

h. Here is the correct shape:

i. The graph that follows includes all of the elements required by the problem:

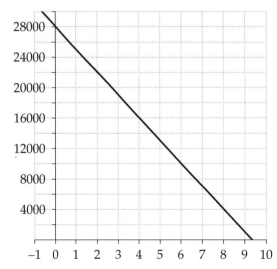

HOMEWORK

1. If the curve started further up on the y-axis, it would mean that the initial value of the motorcycle was higher.
2. If the curve dropped more steeply, it would mean the annual decrease in the motorcycle's value was larger.

Extend the Learning:
Approximately when was the motorcycle worth $14,000?

Answer: The motorcycle was worth $14,000 after approximately four years and eight months.

Value of a Motorcycle
Student Recording Sheet

1. Eight years ago, Derek bought a Ducati motorcycle valued at $28,000. Since then, the value of the motorcycle has decreased steadily by $3,000 each year.

   a. Fill in the table below, which portrays the relationship between value and time since Derek's purchase of the motorcycle.

Time	Value
0	
1	
2	
3	
4	
5	
6	
7	
8	

   b. What are the units of measurement for the first column?

   c. What are the units of measurement for the second column?

   d. Choose a row in the table. Write a sentence about the value of the motorcycle based on the information provided in that row.

   e. How much was the motorcycle worth after seven years?

   f. When was the motorcycle worth $16,000?

g. Is the motorcycle's value changing at a constant rate, more and more quickly, or more and more slowly?

h. If you were to graph the relationship between time and value, which of the following shapes would the curve look like? Circle the correct one.

i. Graph the relationship. Label each axis and provide the scale, indicating the values of the tick marks.

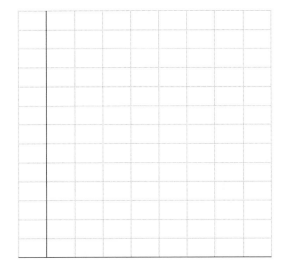

Distance from a House

Given a graph, choose a table; given a table, choose a sentence.

Overview

Class Time: 25 minutes

Prerequisites: Students should have completed Lessons 1.1 through 1.5 and Lessons 2.3 and 3.5.

In this lesson, students learn that for the graph of a linear function, the corresponding table will have a constant rate of change. We want students to develop a strong association between the two.

Teaching the Lesson

In this lesson, students work with a graph and table associated with a linear function. In Section IV, students will be required to come up with equations corresponding to such graphs.

Homework and Assessment

For homework after finishing the recording sheet, ask students to solve this problem:

1. See Tables I, II, and III in the recording sheet, which show distance from an object in terms of time.
   a. How can you tell from a quick look at each table whether the person is walking away from the object or toward the object?
   b. What indicates he or she is standing next to the object at the beginning?

Answers to Lesson 3.6 Student Recording Sheet and Homework

STUDENT RECORDING SHEET

1.
   a. Table III is the correct choice. It is the only table where the change in distance from one second to the next is the same.
   b. The distance covered each second is nine feet.

2.
   a. The sentence that matches the table is Sentence III.
   b.

Table for Sentence I

Time	Distance
0	0
1	4
2	8
3	12
4	16

Table for Sentence II

Time	Distance
0	44
1	36
2	28
3	20
4	12

Table for Sentence IV

Time	Distance
0	0
1	11
2	22
3	33
4	44

HOMEWORK

1.
   a. You should look quickly at the table to see whether the distance is increasing or decreasing over time. If the distance is increasing over time, the person is walking away from the object. If the distance is decreasing over time, the person is walking toward the object.
   b. For the person to be standing next to the object, the first row in the table must have the values of 0 and 0.

Extend the Learning: Draw a time-versus-distance graph like the one in the recording sheet, but provide a different starting distance and a different final time. Also create the table that corresponds to it.

Student _____ Class _____ Date _____

1. Look at the graph below, which shows a man's distance from his house as a function of time. Time in seconds is graphed along the *x*-axis, and distance in feet is graphed along the *y*-axis.

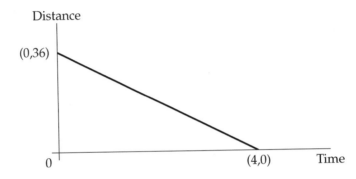

a. Decide which table corresponds with the graph, and explain your choice.

Table I

Time	Distance
0	36
1	30
2	20
3	10
4	0

Table II

Time	Distance
0	36
1	18
2	9
3	3
4	0

(continued)

Table III

Time	Distance
0	36
1	27
2	18
3	9
4	0

b. In the graph/table, how much distance is covered each second?

2. Consider the following table:

Time	Distance from Court
0	44
1	40
2	36
3	32
4	28
11	0

a. From the sentences below, choose one that best matches the table:

Sentence I: An athlete walked away from a tennis court at a rate of four feet per second.

Sentence II: An athlete was forty-four feet away from a tennis court and walked toward it at a rate of eight feet per second.

Sentence III: An athlete was forty-four feet away from a tennis court and walked toward it at a rate of four feet per second.

Sentence IV: An athlete walked away from a tennis court at a rate of eleven feet per second.

b. For each incorrect sentence above, create a table that matches it.

Height of a Projectile

Given a quadratic function, answer questions, and produce a table.

Overview

Class Time: 20 minutes

Prerequisites: Students should have completed Lessons 2.11 and 2.12.

In this lesson, students analyze a quantitative graph describing the height of a projectile as a function of time after it is launched into the air.

Teaching the Lesson

A standard application when studying quadratic functions is to consider the height of a projectile fired directly up into the air as a function of time. It is assumed that the projectile is fired with an initial velocity of v_0 and that no further force is attached to it. Acceleration due to gravity is –32 feet per second squared. Thus, the velocity of the projectile at time t is $v(t) = -32t + v_0$. The height of the projectile above the ground is obtained using a Riemann sum, or the integral that gives us $h(t) = -16t^2 + v_0 t + h_0$, where again, v_0 is the velocity with which the object is projected and h_0 is the initial height of the object.

MATH MATTERS

A *Riemann sum* is a method for approximating the total area underneath a curve on a graph. If the graph represents velocity, this total area represents displacement.

Homework and Assessment

For homework after finishing the recording sheet, ask students to solve this problem: *Suppose a rocket is shot off from the ground and reaches its maximum height of sixty-four feet after two seconds in the air. It is at a height of forty-eight feet after one second and again after three seconds. Make the table and draw the graph of the rocket's height as a function of time.*

Answers to Lesson 3.7 Student Recording Sheet and Homework

STUDENT RECORDING SHEET

1.
   a. The graph shows the relationship between the height of a firework and the time since it was fired into the air.
   b. The units of measurement along the x-axis are likely seconds.
   c. The units of measurement along the y-axis are likely feet.
   d. The firework goes 155 feet into the air.
   e. The firework reaches its maximum height after three seconds.

f. The firework is in the air for a little more than six seconds.
g. The platform is about fifteen feet high.
h. The firework is 120 feet above the ground twice: after 1.5 seconds and 4.5 seconds.
i. After five seconds, the firework is ninety feet in the air.

2.

Time	Height
1	90
2	140
3	155
4	140
5	90
6	8

3. Answers will vary. Here is an example: After five seconds, the firework is ninety feet in the air.

4. The firework was shot off from a platform fifteen feet above the ground. It reached its maximum height of 155 feet after three seconds, and returned to the ground after six seconds.

HOMEWORK

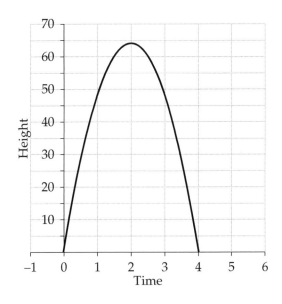

Time	Height
0	0
1	48
2	64
3	48
4	0

Extend the Learning: Look again at the graph on the recording sheet. Imagine drawing a vertical line straight up from 2 on the *x*-axis. What do you notice about the relationship of that line to the curve?

Answer: The line is a line of symmetry. If the graph were folded along this line, all the points on both sides of the curve would match up.

LESSON 3.7 Height of a Projectile
Student Recording Sheet

1. The graph below shows the height of a rocket-type firework over time. The firework is fired from a platform directly into the air, and it falls back to the ground. Study the graph and answer the questions.

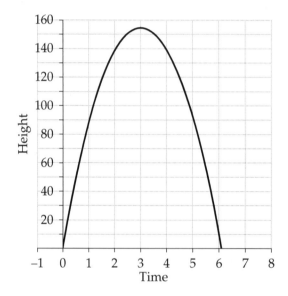

a. This graph shows the relationship between what two quantities?

b. What are the likely units of measurement along the *x*-axis?

c. What are the likely units of measurement along the *y*-axis?

d. How high does the firework go?

e. After how many seconds does the firework reach its maximum height?

f. For how many seconds is the firework in the air?

g. How high is the platform from which the firework is fired?

h. When is the firework 120 feet above the ground?

i. How high is the firework after five seconds?

(continued)

2. Use the points on the curve to fill in Column 2 of this table:

Time	Height
1	
2	
3	
4	
5	
6	

3. Choose a row from the table. Then write a sentence about the firework's height over time using the information provided by that row.

4. Describe the motion of the firework after it was fired into the air.

Throwing a Grapefruit!

Further work with quadratic functions.

Overview

Class Time: 20 minutes

Prerequisites: Students should have experience working with quadratic functions and have completed Lessons 2.11, 2.12, and 3.7.

This lesson, like the previous one, has students work with the height of a projectile in the air as a function of time. This time, however, students are also asked to determine the scales along both axes given one point on the curve.

Teaching the Lesson

As in Lesson 3.7, the formula used to model the motion of a projectile is $h(t) = -16t^2 + v_0t + h_0$, where v_0 is the velocity with which the object was projected and h_0 is the initial height of the object.

Homework and Assessment

For homework after finishing the recording sheet, ask students to solve this problem: *Refer again to the graph on the recording sheet. When is the grapefruit nine feet in the air? Explain why there are two answers to this question.*

Answers to Lesson 3.8 Student Recording Sheet and Homework

STUDENT RECORDING SHEET

1.
  a. The graph shows the relationship between time and height.
  b. The units of measurement along the horizontal axis are likely seconds.
  c. The units of measurement along the vertical axis are likely feet.
  d. After 1 second, the grapefruit is eight feet in the air.
  e. Along the x-axis, where the units of measurement are seconds, the values of the tick marks are 0.2, 0.4, 0.6, 0.8, 1.0, and so on. Along the y-axis, where the units of measurement are feet, the values of the tick marks are 2, 4, 6, 8, and so on.
  f. The grapefruit is thrown into the air from a height of four feet.
  g. The grapefruit reaches a height of just over ten feet.
  h. The grapefruit is in the air for slightly longer than 1.4 seconds.

2.

Time	Height
0	4.2
0.2	7.5
0.4	9.3
0.6	10.3
0.8	9.7
1.0	8.0
1.2	5.0
1.4	0.8

Along the y-axis of the graph, each tick mark represents two feet, so the numbers in the Height column of the table are approximations. Discuss with students how to estimate these values. Note, for instance, that half the distance to a tick mark corresponds to one foot, and half of that distance corresponds to 0.5 foot.

3. Answers will vary. Here is an example: After 0.8 seconds, the grapefruit is 9.7 feet in the air.

HOMEWORK

The grapefruit is nine feet in the air after about 0.3 seconds and again after about 0.9 seconds. There are two answers to this question because the grapefruit reaches 9 feet once on its way up and a second time on its way down.

Extend the Learning: Suppose you are told there is only one answer to the question about what time the grapefruit was at a certain height. At what height or heights is this true?

Answer: It is true at the grapefruit's maximum height, which is reached only once. It is also true if you stand at a height below the height from which the grapefruit was initially thrown into the air.

(continued)

Student _____ Class _____ Date _____

LESSON **3.8** **Throwing a Grapefruit!**
Student Recording Sheet

1. A grapefruit is thrown up in the air. The graph below shows its height as a function of its time in the air.

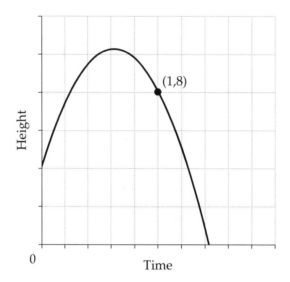

a. This graph shows the relationship between what two quantities?

b. What are the likely units of measurement along the horizontal axis?

c. What are the likely units of measurement along the vertical axis?

d. A point is marked on the curve. Write a sentence about the grapefruit's height over time using the information provided by the coordinates of the point.

(continued)

e. Use the coordinates of the point to determine the scale of each axis. Determine the values of the tick marks along the axes.

f. From what height is the grapefruit thrown into the air?

g. How high does the grapefruit go?

h. For how long is the grapefruit in the air?

2. Use the graph to fill in the table below. Estimate the heights as best you can.

Time	Height

3. Choose a row in the table. Write a sentence about the grapefruit's height over time using the information provided in that row.

Your Choice

Create your own example.

Overview

Class or Homework Time: 15 minutes

Prerequisites: Students should have completed Lesson 3.5.

Here students are given the opportunity to create their own example. A table with eight entries is given and students provide a possible context and graph.

Teaching the Lesson

The lesson can be assigned as homework, done in class, or split between the two (perhaps one question done in class and the others assigned as homework).

For each unit increase in the lefthand column, the entry in the righthand column decreases by 8. Assuming the rate of change for the entire function is constant, we have a decreasing linear function. In the table, we are only given eight points so you may want to point out that drawing a straight line assumes the entire function has a constant rate of change.

Answers will vary. Students should justify their answers. The context should capture the fact that this is a decreasing function starting at a point where the y-value is 48 when the x-value is zero. You may want to point out that the data indicates a straight line but we can't be absolutely sure of that. It is a likely answer but not the only possible answer.

Student _____ Class _____ Date _____

FURTHER PRACTICE **3.A**   **Your Choice**
Create your own example.

Consider the following table.

0	48
1	40
2	32
3	24
4	16
5	8
6	0

1. Think of a situation that this table describes. (Here are two examples. The left-hand column could be time in seconds and the right-hand column distance in feet from a certain object. Using a completely different context, the left-hand column could be time in years and the right-hand column value of an object. You may choose one of these and fill in the details or you may come up with your own example.)

2. Choose a line in the table and write a sentence about the situation using the table entry.

3. Choose a second line in the table and again produce a sentence.

4. Produce a graph that corresponds to the table and the situation. Be careful to make a good decision as to how to put tick marks along the axes.

SECTION IV Adding in Equations

Overview

In this section, the lessons introduce equations. The first seven lessons focus on working with linear relationships. Research has shown that students have trouble understanding that variables vary. They tend to think of variables as particular unknown quantities. Following the approach in this book—in which graphs are introduced before variables—will help improve students' understanding. They will better grasp the concept that the variables stand for the quantities in the relationship depicted and that the quantities take on different values. After students review several examples that lead them from a description of a relationship to an equation, they complete exercises that have them produce an equation, graph, and table representing a particular function.

The last two lessons focus on quadratic functions by considering the height of a rocket over time. This application, which was introduced in Section II and revisited in Section III, is one that students often encounter in high school.

Lessons

LESSON 4.1   **Value of a Computer**   *146*
Work from description, to table, to graph, to equation.

LESSON 4.2   **Purchase of a Jewel**   *150*
Work from graph, to description, to table, to equation for an increasing linear function.

LESSON 4.3   **Distance from a Building**   *153*
Work from graph, to description, to table, to equation for a decreasing linear function.

LESSON 4.4   **Stan Is Waiting**   *157*
Work with a constant function.

LESSON 4.5   **Mary and the Pool**   *160*
Put it all together with an increasing linear function.

LESSON 4.6   **The Cost of Pasta**   *163*
Work from description, to table, to graph, to equation for a cost function.

LESSON 4.7   **Carl at the Gate**   *166*
Put it all together with a decreasing linear function.

LESSON 4.8   **A Rocket in the Air**   *169*
Work from equation, to description, to graph, to table for a quadratic function.

LESSON 4.9   **Another Rocket in the Air**   *174*
Understand quadratic functions.

Value of a Computer

Work from description, to table, to graph, to equation.

Overview

Class Time: 20 minutes

Prerequisites: Students should have completed Lesson 3.5, along with the prerequisites for that lesson.

This lesson introduces the equation associated with a table and a graph. Students will work with a decreasing linear function.

Teaching the Lesson

We have seen that a function can be represented by a description, by a graph, and by a table. When the function is of a special form, it can also be represented by an equation. This lesson begins like one from Section III, but at the end of the lesson, students are required to come up with the equation that corresponds to the function. This lesson should be done by the class as a whole, and Lessons 4.2 and 4.3 should be done by individual students or in small groups.

Homework and Assessment

For homework after finishing the recording sheet, ask students to solve these problems:

Suppose the initial value of a computer was $1,500:

1. How would the table be different?
2. How would the graph be different?
3. How would the equation be different?

Answers to Lesson 4.1 Student Recording Sheet and Homework

STUDENT RECORDING SHEET

1.
   a.

Months	Value
0	$1,200
1	$1,150

Months	Value
2	$1,100
3	$1,050
4	$1,000
5	$950
6	$900
10	$700
15	$450
20	$200

b. Answers will vary. Here is an example sentence: Six months after Joe purchased the computer, it was worth $900.

c. This relationship is a decreasing function. As time passes, the computer is worth less and less.

d. The function is changing at a constant rate: $50 per month.

2.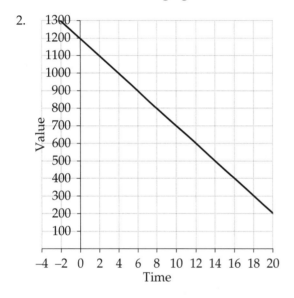

Extend the Learning:
Suppose the original cost of the computer was $1,200 and it decreased in value by $60 a month, rather than $50.
1. How would the table be different?
2. How would the graph be different?
3. How would the equation be different?
Answers:
1. In the table, the Value column would start with $1,200, and each entry would be $60 less than the row above it in the original table.
2. In the graph, the curve would have a steeper slope down than the original curve but the same y-intercept.
3. The equation would be $V = 1,200 - 60M$.

3. $V = 1,200 - 50M$
4. Every line in the table satisfies the equation.
5. Every point on the curve satisfies the equation.

HOMEWORK

1. In the table, the Value column would start with $1,500, rather than $1,200, and each entry would be $300 more than the corresponding entry in the original table.
2. In the graph, the curve would be a line parallel to the original curve, and it would have a y-intercept of $1,500, rather than $1,200.
3. The equation would be $V = 1,500 - 50M$.

Student _____ Class _____ Date _____

1. Joe bought a computer for $1,200 a year and a half ago. Every month since then, its value has gone down by $50.

   a. Fill out the table below, which gives the relationship between the number of months since the purchase of the computer and the computer's value.

Months	Value
0	
1	
2	
3	
4	
5	
6	
7	
8	
9	
10	
15	
20	

   b. Choose a row in the table. Write a sentence about the value of the computer using the information provided in that row.

   c. Is this relationship an increasing or decreasing function?

   d. Is the function changing at a constant rate, faster and faster, or slower and slower?

(continued)

2. Graph the relationship.

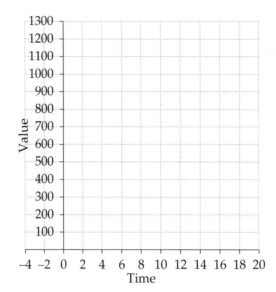

3. Use the following sentence to help you fill in the equation below:

Value (*V*) is the original price minus the decrease per month times the number of months (*M*).

$V = $ _____ $-$ _____ M

4. Take any row in your table, and substitute the first value for *M* and the second value for *V*. Do you get a true statement? Does the equation work for every row in the table? Show your work.

5. Take any point on your graph, and substitute the first coordinate for *M* and the second coordinate for *V*. Do you get a true statement? Does the equation work for every point on the curve? Show your work.

4.2 Purchase of a Jewel

Work from graph, to description, to table, to equation for an increasing linear function.

Overview

Class Time: 20 minutes

Prerequisites: Students should have completed Lessons 3.5 and 4.1.

In this lesson, students start with a graph and are asked to describe the relationship it represents in as much detail as possible. Then they create a table using the y-intercept and the rate of change shown in the graph. Finally, they produce the corresponding equation.

Teaching the Lesson

In Lesson 4.1, students started with a description, filled in a table, created a graph, and then produced an equation. These are all the ways commonly used to represent a function. In this lesson, students work with the same four representations but in a different order. The variables most commonly used to represent values along the axes are x and y, and we use those here.

Homework and Assessment

For homework after finishing the recording sheet, ask students to solve these problems:

1. How would the graph be different if the purchase price of the jewel was changed?
2. How would the graph be different if the value of the jewel rose by $500 a year?

Answers to Lesson 4.2 Student Recording Sheet and Homework

STUDENT RECORDING SHEET

1.
   a. The jewel was purchased for $2,000. It increased in value at a steady rate and was worth $3,200 after three years.
   b. The value of the jewel is increasing by $400 a year.

2.

Time (x)	Value (y)
0	$2,000
1	$2,400
2	$2,800
3	$3,200
4	$3,600

3. $y = 2,000 + 400x$
4. Answers will vary. Here is an example sentence: After three years, the jewel was worth $3,200.
5. Answers will vary. Here is an example sentence: After four years, the jewel was worth $3,600.

HOMEWORK

1. The y-intercept would be higher than that of the original graph.
2. The curve would have a steeper slope than that of the original graph.

Extend the Learning: Suppose the value of the jewel increased faster and faster over the years. How would the graph be different?
Answer: The curve would not be a straight line. Its shape would be concave up:

Student _____ Class _____ Date _____

1. Consider the graph below, which shows the value of a jewel as a function of time since its purchase. Time in years is shown along the *x*-axis, and value in dollars is shown along the *y*-axis.

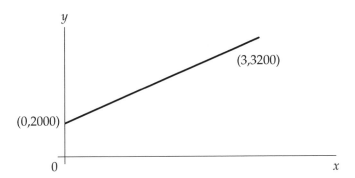

   a. Describe the relationship shown by the graph in as much detail as possible.

   b. How fast is the value of the jewel increasing? (Be sure to include units.)

2. Complete the table by filling in the blanks.

Time (x)	Value (y)
0	
1	
2	
3	
4	

3. Write a formula to describe the value of the jewel (*y*) after *x* years. To do so, translate into symbols the beginning value plus the increase in value per year times the number of years.

4. Choose a point on the graph, and write a sentence about the jewel's value based on the information provided by the coordinates.

5. Choose a row in the table, and write a sentence about the jewel's value based on the information provided in that row.

From *It's All Connected: The Power of Representation to Build Algebraic Reasoning, Grades 6–9* by Frances Van Dyke. © 2012 by Scholastic Inc. Permission granted to photocopy for nonprofit use in a classroom or similar place dedicated to face-to-face educational purposes. Downloadable at www.mathsolutions.com/itsallconnectedalgebrareproducibles.

Distance from a Building

Work from graph, to description, to table, to equation for a decreasing linear function.

Overview

Class Time: 20 minutes

Prerequisites: Students should have completed Lessons 3.5, 4.1, and 4.2.

In this lesson, the function is decreasing, rather than increasing. After describing the relationship as well as they can, students are asked to fill in a table using the rate of change and y-intercept represented in the graph. Then they create an equation based on the description and table corresponding to the relationship.

Teaching the Lesson

As in Lesson 4.2, students work with the same four representations of information: description, graph, table, and equation. They start by interpreting the graph. Describing the relationship in words based on the graph is an exercise not often seen in textbooks. It is designed to help students become more comfortable with graphs. Too often students think of graphs as an exercise associated with an equation and do not view them as an equal partner for representing a function.

Homework and Assessment

For homework after finishing the recording sheet, ask students to solve these problems:

1. How would changing the initial distance make the graph different?
2. Suppose the man is walking away from the building. How will the graph be different?

Answers to Lesson 4.3 Student Recording Sheet and Homework

STUDENT RECORDING SHEET

1.
   a. The man starts twenty-four feet from the building, and he reaches the building after six seconds.
   b. The man is walking at a pace of four feet per second.

2.

Time (x)	Distance (y)
0	24
1	20
1.5	18
2	16
2.5	14
3	12
4	8
4.5	6
5	4
6	0

3. $y = 24 - 4x$
4. Answers will vary. Here is an example sentence: After six seconds, the man is at the building.
5. Answers will vary. Here is an example sentence: After three seconds, the man is four feet from the building.
6. The x-intercept represents the time it takes the man to reach the building, and the y-intercept represents the man's initial distance from the building.

HOMEWORK

1. Changing the initial distance would make the y-intercept different from that of the original graph.
2. The function of the new graph will be increasing, not decreasing.

Extend the Learning: Suppose the man walks slower and slower. How will the graph be different? **Answer:** The curve will not be a straight line. Its shape will be concave up:

From *It's All Connected: The Power of Representation to Build Algebraic Reasoning, Grades 6–9* by Frances Van Dyke. © 2012 by Scholastic Inc.
Permission granted to photocopy for nonprofit use in a classroom or similar place dedicated to face-to-face educational purposes.
Downloadable at www.mathsolutions.com/itsallconnectedalgebrareproducibles.

LESSON 4.3 — Distance from a Building
Student Recording Sheet

1. Consider the graph below, which shows a man's distance from a building as a function of time in seconds. Time in seconds is graphed along the *x*-axis, and distance in feet is graphed along the *y*-axis.

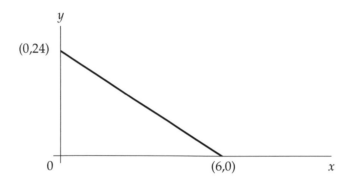

   a. Describe the situation in as much detail as possible.

   b. How fast is the man walking? Be sure to include the units.

2. Complete the table below, filling in the blanks and adding more entries.

Time (x)	Distance (y)
0	
1	24 − 4(1)
1.5	24 − 4( )
	24 − 4(2)
2	
3	
4	

3. Create a formula to describe how far away the man is after *x* seconds, where *x* is any time between the beginning of the walk and the end of the walk. To do so, translate into symbols that the man's distance equals the initial distance minus the rate times the time.

(continued)

Emotional development, 42–43
Emotional intelligence, 203–210
    forming friendships, 201–202
    infatuation, 204–205
    interpersonal conflict, 206–210
    mature love, 205–206
Empirical evidence, citing, 179
Employability, 37–40
*Encyclopedia of Careers and Vocational
    Guidance*, 285
English composition, 34
Essay questions, 131–134
Ethical development, 42, 44, 325
Ethnic diversity, 231
Ethnic group, defined, 228–229
Evaluation, 78
Exam-taking skills, 123–143
    anxiety, exam, 136–138
    essay questions, 131–134
    during exam strategies, 127–128
    lost points on exams, source of,
        135–136
    multiple choice questions, 128–130
    post-exam strategies, 135
    pre-exam strategies, 123–127
    recitation, 124–125
    retrieval cues, 125–126
Exams
    anxiety, 136–138
    lost points on, source of, 135–136
    recalling questions, 124
    recognition of questions, 124
    results-review teams, 18
Exercise, 215, 331–335
    benefits for body, 331–332
    benefits for mind, 333
    effectiveness of, 333–335
Existential intelligence, 254
Externship programs, 286
Extraversion, 255–256

F

Faculty members, interaction with,
    11–13
Failure, fear of, 85
Familiarity, appealing to, 181
Family perspective, 48
Fear of failure, 85
Fear of success, 85
Federal loans, private, contrasted, 312
Federal Perkins Loan, 311
Federal Student Aid, application for,
    309–310
Federal Subsidized Stafford Loan, 311
Federal Unsubsidized Stafford Loan,
    311

Final draft, 17
Financial aid counselors, 14
Financial aid office, 10
Fine arts, 34
First draft, 17
Fiscal planning, 303–324
    cash flow, 305–309
    charge card, 308
    checking account, 305–306
    credit card, 306–308
    debit card, 308–309
    federal loans, private, contrasted, 312
    Federal Student Aid, application for,
        309–310
    financial self-awareness, 304
    grants, 311
    income sources, 309–316
    loans, 311–312
    money-management plan, 305
    money-saving habits, 313–316
    salary earnings, 312–313
    scholarships, 311
Fitness, 331–335
Food, sleep-interfering, 338
Forms of higher-level thinking, 174
Forms of intelligence, 254
Futuristic perspective, 50–51

G

Generality, 180
Generalization, 180
Genocide, 239
Geographical perspective, 177
Geography, 35
Geology, 35
Glittering generality, 180
Global perspective, 49
Goal setting, 58–59
    long-range goals, setting, 59
    personal abilities, talents, 61
    personal interests, 60–61
    personal values, 61–62
    self-awareness, 60–62
    SMART method, 64
    steps in process, 59–64
    strategies for, 58–59
Grants, 311
Gravity, 77

H

Habits, learning, 21
Hallucinogens, 344
Harassment
    nonverbal, 342
    physical, 342

sexual, 342–343
verbal, 343
Hasty generalization, 180
Hate crimes, 239
Hate groups, 239
Health, 325–351
    alcohol, 339–348
    drugs, 339–348
    eating disorders, 329
    exercise, 331–335
    fitness, 331–335
    nutrition, 328–331
    physical wellness, elements of,
        327–328
    rest, 335–338
    risky behavior, 335–348
    sexual harassment, 342–343
    sexually transmitted infections, 348
    sleep, 335–338
    unhealthy relationships, 341–344
    wellness, defining, 325–327
Health center, 10
Heroin, use of, 344
Hierarchy of needs, 15
High-fat foods, 338
Higher-level thinking, 173–195
    analytical thinking, 175
    applied thinking, 175
    balanced thinking, 181–183
    creative thinking, 184–185
    critical thinking, 183–184
    defined, 173–174
    developing, 185–190
    forms of, 174–185
    inferential reasoning, 179–181
    logical fallacies, 180–181
    multidimensional thinking, 176–178
    synthesis, 175–176
Historical perspective, 50
History, 35
Holistic development, skills associated
    with, 42–48
Human relations skills, 200
Humanities, 34
Humanity, 231
    defining, 230–231
Humor, importance of, 215

I

Idealism, 204
Income sources, 309–316
    federal, private loans, contrasted, 312
    Federal Student Aid, application for,
        309–310
    grants, 311
    loans, 311–312

money-saving habits, 313–316
salary earnings, 312–313
scholarships, 311
Indecisiveness, 85
Index as information tool, 147
Individuality, 231
defining, 231
Infatuation, 204–205
Inferential reasoning, 179–181
errors, 180–181
Information interviews, 286
Information literacy, 145–171
citing research sources, 151–153
credibility of sources, evaluating,
148–149
plagiarism, 152–153
quality of sources, evaluating,
148–149
quantity of sources, evaluating,
149–150
reference sources, 145–148
reference styles, 151
research sources, 150
variety of sources, evaluating,
149–150
Information-search tools
abstract, 147
catalog, 147
citation, 147
database, 147
descriptor, 147
index, 147
keyword, 147
search engine, 147
search thesaurus, 147
subscription database, 147
Uniform Resource Locator, 147
wildcard, 147
Information tools
abstract, 147
catalog, 147
citation, 147
database, 147
descriptor, 147
index, 147
keyword, 147
search engine, 147
search thesaurus, 147
subscription database, 147
Uniform Resource Locator, 147
wildcard, 147
Institutional racism, 238
Integration, 112
Intellectual development, 42–43

Intelligence
existential, 254
forms of, 254
interpersonal, 254
intrapersonal, 254
linguistic, 254
logical-mathematical, 254
musical, 254
naturalist, 254
spatial, 254
Intelligences, multiple, 253–254
Interacting with diverse students,
240–242
Interaction, interpersonal, 11–20
academic advisors, 13–14
collaboration with peers, 16
faculty members, interaction with,
11–13
learning communities, 18–20
library research teams, 17
mentors, interaction with, 14
note-taking teams, 16–17
with peers, 14–16
reading, teams, 17
study teams, 18
team-instructor conferences, 17–18
test results-review teams, 18
writing teams, 17
Interaction with mentors, 14
Interests
college major, compatibility with,
263–268
personal, 60
International diversity, 232–233
International perspective, 49
Internships, 287
Interpersonal communication, 198–200
Interpersonal conflict, 206–210
Interpersonal intelligence, 254
Interpersonal interaction, 11–20
academic advisors, 13–14
assignment-review teams, 18
collaboration with peers, 16
faculty members, interaction with,
11–13
learning communities, 18–20
library research teams, 17
mentors, interaction with, 14
note-taking teams, 16–17
with peers, 14–16
reading teams, 17
study teams, 18
team-instructor conferences, 17–18
test results-review teams, 18
writing teams, 17

Interviews, 286
Intrapersonal intelligence, 254
Intraversion, 255–256
Involvement, 2–7
active class participation, 5–6
active listening, 3–5
active reading, 6–7
class attendance, 3
note taking, 3–5
time spent in class, 3
time spent on coursework outside
classroom, 3

J

Jealousy, 205
Jim Crow laws, 238
Job shadowing programs, 286
Journal, 215
Jumping to conclusion, 180
Jung, Carl, 255

K

Keyword, 147

L

Languages, 34
Large, stable calendar, 77
Laughter, importance of, 215
Learning
stages in, 95–96
writing for, 154–156
Learning center, 8
Learning communities, 18–20
Learning from diversity, 238–239
Learning habits, 21
Learning styles, 21, 254–259
Learning Styles Inventory, 257
Myers-Briggs Type Indicator, 256
Lecture-listening, 96–102
post-lecture strategies, 102
pre-lecture strategies, 96–99
Letters of recommendation, 297–298
Liberal arts education, 31–56
behavioral science, 35
chronological perspective, elements
of, 50–51
co-curriculum, 46–48
community perspective, 48
cultural perspective, 49
curriculum, 32–33
divisions of knowledge, 33–36
employability, 37–40
family perspective, 48
fine arts, 34

futuristic perspective, 50–51
global perspective, 49
historical perspective, 50
holistic development, skills associated with, 42–48
humanities, 34
international perspective, 49
knowledge divisions, 33–36
mathematics, 34
meaning, 32
national perspective, 49
natural sciences, 35
physical education, 36
purpose, 32
self, dimensions of, 42–43
self-awareness, 41–42
social science, 35
social-spatial perspective, 48–50
societal perspective, 48
subject areas, 33–36
synoptic perspective, 51
transferable skills, acquiring, 37–42
university perspective, 50
wellness education, 36
Library research teams, 17
Lifelong learning skills, 40
Linguistic intelligence, 254
Linguistic perspective, 177
Listening, writing for, 154
Listening skills, 198
Literacy, information, 145–171
plagiarism, 152–153
reference sources, 145–148
reference styles, 151
Literature, 34
Loans, 311–312
federal, private, contrasted, 312
Federal Perkins, 311
Federal Subsidized Stafford, 311
Federal Unsubsidized Stafford, 311
Logical consistency, 179
Logical fallacies, 180–181
Logical-mathematical intelligence, 254
Long-range educational planning, 252–263
Long-range goals, setting, 59
Long-range plan, 79
Lost points on exams, source of, 135–136
Love, mature, 205–206
Love sickness, 205

M

Major, 249–250
career, relationship, 260–263
choice of, 251–259
college, 249–250, 252–259
compatibility with interests, 263–268
factors to consider, 252–259
Management of time, 75–93
action plan, 82
elements of plan, 78–82
importance of, 75–82
Murphy's laws, 80
plan, 78
procrastination, 83–88
strategies, 76–78
Map of concepts, 158
Marijuana, 344
Marketing, 293–294
Maslow, Abraham, hierarchy of needs, 15
Mathematics, 34
Mature love, 205–206
MBTI. *See* Myers-Briggs Type Indicator
Meeting people, 201–202
Memory block, 128
Memory process, stages in, 95–96
Memory retrieval, 95
Memory storage, 95
Mental imagery, 214–215
Mentors, interaction with, 14
Mid-range plan, 79
Minister, chaplain, interaction with, 14
Money management, 303–324
cash flow, 305–309
charge card, 308
checking account, 305–306
credit card, 306–308
debit card, 308–309
federal loans, private, contrasted, 312
Federal Student Aid, application for, 309–310
financial self-awareness, 304
grants, 311
income sources, 309–316
loans, 311–312
money-management plan, 305
money-saving habits, 313–316
salary earnings, 312–313
scholarships, 311
Money-management plan, 305
Money-saving habits, 313–316
Motivation, 64–67
Movement, bodily-kinesthetic, 254
Moving, learning by, 117
Multidimensional thinking, 176–178
perspectives associated with, 177
Multiple choice questions, 128–130
Multiple intelligences, 253–254
Murphy's laws, 80
Muscle relaxation, 214

Musical arts, 34
Musical intelligence, 254
Myers-Briggs Type Indicator, 255–256
learning styles, 256
Myths promoting procrastination, 83–84

N

Narcotics, 344
National perspective, 49
Natural sciences, 35
Naturalist intelligence, 254
Needs hierarchy, Maslow's, 15
Nicotine, 338
Nonverbal cues, 100
Nonverbal harassment, 342
Note taking, 3–5, 96–102
post-lecture strategies, 102
pre-lecture strategies, 96–99
Note-taking teams, 16–17
Nutrition, 36, 328–331
eating disorders, 329

O

Objectivity, 149
Occupational development, 325
Occupational Information Network, 285
Office of student life, 9
OIN. *See* Occupational Information Network
Oral presentations, 162–168
importance of, 162–163
making, 163–168
PowerPoint, 165
speech anxiety, reducing, 166
Organization, 112
Organizing, writing for, 155

P

Papers, writing, 156–162
Part-time work, 289–290
Part-to-whole study method, 113
PDA. *See* Personal digital assistant
Peer collaboration
reading, teams, 17
team-instructor conferences, 17–18
Peers
collaboration with, 16
interaction with, 14–16
library research teams, 17
note-taking teams, 16–17
study teams, 18
test results-review teams, 18
writing teams, 17

People skills, 200
Perception, selective, 180
Perfectionism, 85
Performing arts, 34
Personal abilities, 21
    talents, 61
Personal character, importance of,
    68–69
Personal development, 42, 45, 325
Personal digital assistant, 76
Personal interests, 21, 60–61
    college major, compatibility with,
    263–268
Personal reflection, 20–24
    self-assessment, 21–22
    self-monitoring, 22–24
Personal resume, 296–297
Personal technology, use in classroom,
    13
Personal values, 21, 61–62
Personality traits, 22
Perspectives associated with
    multidimensional thinking, 177
Philosophical perspective, 177
Philosophy, 34
Phones, use in classroom, 13
Physical development, 42, 44
Physical education, 36
Physical harassment, 342
Physical wellness, elements of, 327–328
Physics, 35
Plagiarism, 152–153
Plan
    long-range, 79
    mid-range, 79
    short-range, 79
Planning, educational, 249–277
    career, relationship, 260–263
    college major, 249–250
    compatibility with interests, 263–268
    intelligence, forms of, 254
    learning styles, 254–259
    Learning Styles Inventory, learning
    styles, 257
    long-range educational planning,
    252–263
    multiple intelligences, 253–254
    Myers-Briggs Type Indicator,
    255–256
Political perspective, 177
Political science, 35
Portable planner, 76
Portfolio, personal, 294–295
Possessiveness, 205
Post-lecture strategies, 102

Post-reading strategies, 107–109
Post-test strategies, 135
PowerPoint presentations, 165
Pre-lecture strategies, 96–99
Pre-reading strategies, 103–104
Pre-test strategies, 123–127
    recitation, 124–125
    retrieval cues, 125–126
Pre-writing, 17
Prejudice, 237–238
Prescription pain pills, use of, 344
Prestige, appealing to, 181
Principles of college success, 1–2
Prioritizing, 76
Private loans, federal, contrasted, 312
Problem solving, writing for, 156
Procrastination, 83–88
    defined, 83
    myths promoting, 83–84
    psychological causes, 84–85
    self-help strategies, 85–88
Progress toward goals, 64–67
Psychedelics, use of, 344
Psychological causes, procrastination,
    84–85
Psychological perspective, 177
Psychology, 35
Psychomotor movement, 254
Public speaking, 162–168
    importance of, 162–163
    PowerPoint, 165
    speech anxiety, reducing, 166

Q

Quality of sources, evaluating, 148–149
Quantity of references, 149–150
Quantity of sources, evaluating,
    149–150

R

Race, defining, 225–227
Racial diversity, 231
Racism, 238
    institutional, 238
Reading, writing for, 154
Reading comprehension/retention,
    SQ3R method, 108
Reading strategies, 103–109
    post-reading strategies, 107–109
    pre-reading strategies, 103–104
    SQ3R, 108
    strategies to use while reading,
    104–106
Reasoning, circular, 180–181

Recalling test questions, 124
Recitation, 124–125
Recognition test questions, 124
Recommendation, letters of, 297–298
Red herring, 180
Reference letters, 297–298
Reference sources, 145–148
    citing, 151–153
    credibility of, evaluating, 148–149
    as inspiration, 150
    quality of, evaluating, 148–149
Reference styles, 151
    American Psychological Association,
    151
    Modern Language Association, 151
References
    quantity of, 149–150
    variety of, 150
Refinement of topic, 17
Reflection, personal, 20–24
    self-assessment, 21–22
    self-monitoring, 22–24
Relationships, unhealthy, 341–344
Religious bigotry, 239
Remembering, writing for, 154
Reports, writing, 156–162
Research skills, 145
Research sources
    citing, 151–153
    use as inspiration, 150
Resources, campus, 7–11
    academic advising center, 9
    academic support center, 8
    career development center, 10–11
    college library, 8–9
    counseling center, 10
    disability services, 8
    financial aid office, 10
    health center, 10
    office of student life, 9
    writing center, 8
Resources on careers, 284–285
Rest, 335–338
Resume, personal, 296–297
Retention/comprehension, SQ3R
    method, 108
Retrieval, memory, 95
Retrieval cues, 125–126
Rhetorical deception, 180
Risky behavior, 335–348
Romantic relationships, 203–210
    infatuation, 204–205
    interpersonal conflict, 206–210
    mature love, 205–206

S

Salary earnings, 312–313
Scholarly perspective, 148
Scholarships, 311
Science, political, 35
Scientific perspective, 177
Search engine, 147
Search thesaurus, 147
Search tools
  abstract, 147
  catalog, 147
  citation, 147
  database, 147
  descriptor, 147
  index, 147
  keyword, 147
  search engine, 147
  search thesaurus, 147
  subscription database, 147
  Uniform Resource Locator, 147
  wildcard, 147
Segregation, 238
Selective perception, 180
Self, dimensions of, 42–43
Self-assessment, 21–22
Self-awareness, 41–42, 60–62
Self-concept, academic, 22
Self-help strategies
  to combat procrastination, 85–88
  procrastination, 85–88
Self-marketing, 293–294
Self-monitored learning, 118–120
Self-monitoring, 22–24, 291–293
Sensory input, 95
Service learning, 288–289
Setting goals, SMART method, 64
Sexual abuse, 342–344
Sexual assault, 343
Sexual harassment, 342–343
Sexuality, 36
Sexually transmitted infections, 348
Shadowing, 286–287
Short-range plan, 79
Slavery, 238
Sleep
  importance of, 336
  purpose of, 335
  quality, 336–338
Sleep-interfering beverages, 338
Sleep-interfering foods, beverages, 338
Slippery slope, 180
SMART method of goal setting, 64
Smoke screen, 180
Social development, 42–44, 325
  forming friendships, 201–202

Social intelligence, 197–202, 254
  human relations skills, 200
  interpersonal communication,
    198–200
  meeting people, 201–202
Social science, 35
Social-spatial perspective, 48–50
  community perspective, 48
  cultural perspective, 49
  family perspective, 48
  global perspective, 49
  international perspective, 49
  national perspective, 49
  societal perspective, 48
  university perspective, 50
Societal perspective, 48
Socioeconomic diversity, 232
Sociological perspective, 177
Sociology, 35
Sources
  citing, 151–153
  credibility of, evaluating, 148–149
  quality of, evaluating, 148–149
  use as inspiration, 150
Spatial intelligence, 254
Speech anxiety, reducing, 166
Speeches, 162–168
  importance of, 162–163
  making, 163–168
  PowerPoint, 165
  speech anxiety, reducing, 166
Spiritual development, 42, 44–45, 325
SQ3R method, reading comprehension/
    retention, 108
Standard, double, 180
Statistics, 34
Stereotypes, 235–238
Stereotyping, 238
STIs. *See* Sexually transmitted infections
Storage, memory, 95
Strategies to use while reading, 104–106
Straw man argument, 180
Stress, 211–215
Stress management, 213–216
  diaphragmatic breathing, 214
  mental imagery, 214–215
  muscle relaxation, 214
Student-student interaction, 14–16
Study process, variety in, 115
Study strategies, 109–120
  associations, 110–111
  attention, 109–118
  comparing/contrasting, 111–112
  contrasting, 111–112
  dividing material, 112–113
  integration, 112

  organization, 112
  part-to-whole study method, 113
  self-monitored learning, 118–120
  undivided attention, 109–118
  variety in study process, 113–118
Study teams, 18
Studying, writing for, 155
Styles of learning, 21, 254–259
  Learning Styles Inventory, 257
  Myers-Briggs Type Indicator, 256
Subject areas, liberal arts education,
    33–36
Subscription database, 147
Success
  defining, 57–58
  fear of, 85
Success diamond, 2
Symptoms of anxiety, 213
Synoptic perspective, 51
Synthesis, 78, 175–176

T

Talents, 60
Teams
  library research, 17
  note-taking, 16–17
  study, 18
  test results-review, 18
  writing, 17
Technology, personal, in classroom, 13
Test-taking skills, 123–143
  anxiety, test, 136–138
  essay questions, 131–134
  lost points on exams, source of,
    135–136
  multiple choice questions, 128–130
  post-test strategies, 135
  pre-test strategies, 123–127
  recitation, 124–125
  retrieval cues, 125–126
  during test strategies, 127–128
Tests
  anxiety, 136–138
  lost points on, source of, 135–136
  recalling questions, 124
  recognition of questions, 124
  results-review teams, 18
Text messaging in classroom, 13
Theological perspective, 177
Theology, 34
Thesaurus, 147
Thinking skills, 40
Thrill seeking, 85
Time management, 75–93
  elements of plan, 78–82
  importance of, 75–82

Murphy's laws, 80
plan, 78
plan for, 82
procrastination, 83–88
strategies, 76–78
Time spent in class, 3
Time spent on coursework outside
    classroom, 3
Tone of voice cues, 100
Topic selection, 17
Tradition, appealing to, 181
Traits, personality, 22
Transcript, course, 294
Transferable skills, acquiring, 37–42
Types of diversity, 231–233

U

Understanding, writing for, 155
Undivided attention, 109–118
Unhealthy relationships, 341–344
Uniform Resource Locator, 147
University perspective, 50
URL. *See* Uniform Resource Locator

V

Values, 60
    personal, 21
Variety in study process, 113–118
Variety of references, 150
Variety of sources, evaluating, 149–150
Verbal cues, 100
Verbal harassment, 343
Violence, sexual, 342–344
Visual arts, 34
Visual learning, 115
Vocabulary, college, 361–365
Vocational development, 42, 45, 325
Volunteer work, 288–289

W

Wellness, 325–351
    alcohol, 339–348
    alcohol and aggressive behaviors,
        341–344
    alcohol and drugs, 347–348
    defining, 325–327
    drugs, 339–348
    eating disorders, 329
    exercise, 331–335

fitness, 331–335
    nutrition, 328–331
    physical wellness, elements of,
        327–328
    relevance of, 327
    rest, 335–338
    risky behavior, 335–348
    sexual harassment, 342–343
    sexually transmitted infections, 348
    sleep, 335–338
    unhealthy relationships, 341–344
Wellness education, 36
Whole-person development, 42–48
Wildcard, 147
Wishful thinking, 180
Writing center, 8
Writing papers, 156–162
Writing skills, 153–162
    power of writing, 153
Writing styles, Myers-Briggs Type
    Indicator, 256
Writing teams, 17

X

Xenophobia, 239

4. Choose a point on the graph, and write a sentence about the man's distance based on the information provided by the coordinates.

5. Choose a row in the table, and write a sentence about the man's distance based on the information provided in that row.

6. What information is provided by the *x*- and *y*-intercepts?

Stan Is Waiting

Work with a constant function.

Overview

Class Time: 15 minutes

Prerequisites: Students should have knowledge of constant functions (see Lesson 3.2).

This lesson brings together all the representations—description, graph, table, and equation—and connects them with arrows. This format will be used for the remaining exercises in Section IV. Because the representations look so different, students tend to forget the underlying equivalence that these are all depicting the same function. The double-headed arrows reinforce this idea. In this lesson, the statement is given and the remaining three representations must be provided by the student.

Teaching the Lesson

Have students discuss the different representations as a group and write up the results independently. Because the representations look so different, students tend to forget their underlying equivalence. Reinforce the concept that all the representations depict the same function.

Homework and Assessment

For homework after finishing the recording sheet, ask students to solve these problems:

1. How would the graph be different if Stan walked toward the fence?
2. How would the table be different if Stan walked toward the fence?
3. How would the graph be different if Stan walked away from the fence?
4. How would the table be different if Stan walked away from the fence?

STUDENT RECORDING SHEET

1.

Statement: Stan stood nine feet from the fence and waited.

Table

Time (x)	Distance (y)
0	9
1	9
2	9
3	9
.	.
.	.
.	.
12	9

Graph

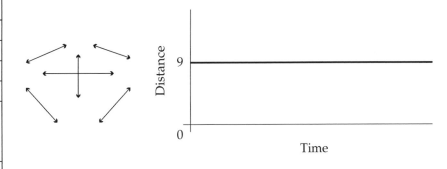

Equation: $y = 9$

2. We have chosen to find values for each unit of time. The units of measurement along the y-axis are feet.
3. After three minutes, Stan was still standing nine feet from the fence.

HOMEWORK

1. As time passed, Sam's distance from the fence would decrease, so the graph would show a decreasing function. If Sam walked at steady pace, then the function would be linear.
2. The Time column could stay the same, but the Distance column would contain decreasing values.
3. As time passed, Sam's distance from the fence would increase, so the graph would show an increasing function. If Sam walked at a steady pace, then the function would be linear.
4. The Time column could stay the same, but the Distance column would contain increasing values.

Extend the Learning:
1. Suppose Stan walked away from the fence at a rate of two feet per second. Write the equation to describe this situation.
2. Suppose Stan walked toward the fence at a rate of three feet per second. Write the equation to describe this situation.
Answers:
1. $y = 9 + 2x$
2. $y = 9 - 3x$

LESSON 4.4 Stan Is Waiting
Student Recording Sheet

1. Given the statement below, create a table, graph, and equation that represent Stan's distance from the fence in terms of time. (Be sure to label the axes of the graph and the columns of the table.)

Statement: Stan stood 9 feet from the fence and waited.

Table   **Graph**

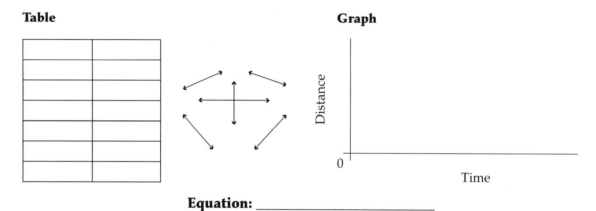

Equation: _____

2. What are the units of measurement along the *x*-axis? What are the units of measurement along the *y*-axis?

3. Choose a row in the table, and write a statement about the application based on the information provided in that row.

LESSON 4.5

Mary and the Pool

Put it all together with an increasing linear function.

Overview

Class Time: 15 minutes

Prerequisites: Students should have knowledge of linear functions (see Lessons 4.1 through 4.3).

Like Lesson 4.4, this lesson brings together all the representations—description, graph, table, and equation—and connects them with double-headed arrows. The relationship is a linear increasing function. This chapter helps students form linear equations from descriptions while keeping them closely associated to their corresponding tables and graphs.

Teaching the Lesson

Because the representations look so different, students tend to forget their underlying equivalence. Once again, emphasize that they are all representations of the same information.

Homework and Assessment

For homework after finishing the recording sheet, ask students to solve these problems:

1. How long did it take Mary to get twenty-five feet from the pool?
2. How long did it take Mary to get thirty feet from the pool?

STUDENT RECORDING SHEET

1.

Statement: Mary was five feet from the pool and started walking away from it at a rate of two feet per second.

Table

Time (x)	Distance (y)
0	5
1	7
2	9
3	11
.	.
.	.
.	.
12	29

Graph

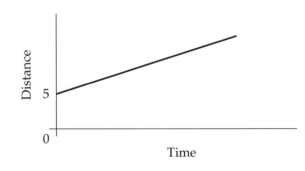

Equation: $y = 5 + 2x$

2. We chose to record the units of measurement along the *x*-axis in seconds. The units of measurement along the *y*-axis are feet.
3. Answers will vary. Here is an example sentence: After three seconds, Mary was eleven feet from the pool.
4. The *y*-intercept tells Mary's initial distance from the pool.

HOMEWORK

1. It took Mary ten seconds to get twenty-five feet from the pool.
2. It took Mary twelve and a half seconds to get thirty feet from the pool.

Extend the Learning: If Mary started twenty-five feet from the pool and walked toward it at a rate of three feet per second, how long would it take her to reach the pool?
Answer: It would take Mary 8.33 seconds to reach the pool.

LESSON **4.5** **Mary and the Pool**
Student Recording Sheet

1. Given the statement below, create a table, graph, and equation that represent Mary's distance from the pool in terms of time. (Be sure to label the axes of the graph and the columns of the table.)

Statement: Mary was five feet from the pool and started walking away from it at a rate of two feet per second.

Table

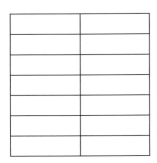

Graph

Equation: _____

2. What are the likely units of measurement along the *x*-axis? What are the units of measurement along the *y*-axis?

3. Choose a row in the table, and write a statement about the application based on the information provided in that row.

4. What information is provided by the *y*-intercept?

The Cost of Pasta

Work from description, to table, to graph, to equation for a cost function.

Overview

Class Time: 15 minutes

Prerequisites: Students should have completed Lessons 4.1 through 4.3.

Like Lesson 4.5, this lesson reinforces the underlying equivalence of the statement, graph, table, and equation for an increasing linear function.

Teaching the Lesson

In the majority of lessons in this book, time is the independent variable. Here it is the number of pounds of pasta purchased. Point this out to the students and ask about the significance of the y-intercept and the slope. The units of the slope are always the units of y divided by the units of x. Ask students what the units of the slope are (dollars per pound).

Homework and Assessment

For homework after finishing the recording sheet, ask students to solve these problems:

1. How much does seventeen pounds of pasta cost? What point on the graph corresponds to this amount and cost of pasta? Provide the coordinates.
2. How many pounds of pasta can be purchased for thirty dollars? What point on the graph corresponds to this amount and cost of pasta? Provide the coordinates.

STUDENT RECORDING SHEET

1.

Statement: Pasta costs sixty cents a pound.

Table

Pounds	Cost
1	$0.60
2	$1.20
3	$1.80
4	$2.40
5	$3.00

Graph

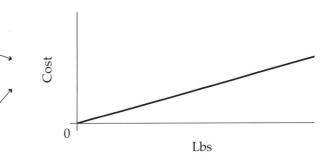

Equation: $y = 6x$

2. Whole numbers have been chosen for the first column of the table. The units of measurement along the x-axis are pounds. The units of measurement along the y-axis are dollars.

3. Answers will vary. Here is an example sentence: The cost of four pounds of pasta is $2.40.

HOMEWORK

1. Seventeen pounds of pasta costs $10.20. The corresponding point on the graph is (17,10.2).

2. Fifty pounds of pasta can be purchased for thirty dollars. The corresponding point on the graph is (50,30).

> **Extend the Learning:** Make up a problem of this type to give to your classmate. Provide an answer key. **Answer:** Students' problems should involve creating all four representations: statement, graph, table, and equation.

From *It's All Connected: The Power of Representation to Build Algebraic Reasoning, Grades 6–9* by Frances Van Dyke. © 2012 by Scholastic Inc. Permission granted to photocopy for nonprofit use in a classroom or similar place dedicated to face-to-face educational purposes. Downloadable at www.mathsolutions.com/itsallconnectedalgebrareproducibles.

LESSON 4.6 The Cost of Pasta
Student Recording Sheet

1. Given the statement below, create a table, graph, and equation that represent the cost of pasta in terms of the number of pounds purchased. (Be sure to label the axes of the graph and the columns of the table.)

Statement: Pasta costs 60 cents a pound.

Table **Graph**

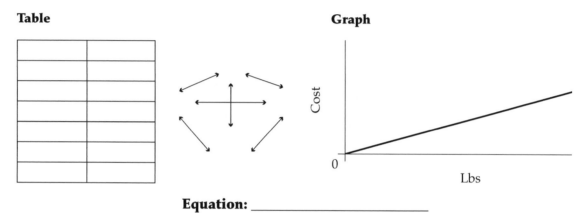

Equation: _____

2. What are the units of measurement along the *x*-axis? What are the units of measurement along the *y*-axis?

3. Choose a row in the table, and write a statement about the application based on the information provided in that row.

Carl at the Gate

Put it all together with a decreasing linear function.

Overview

Class Time: 15 minutes

Prerequisites: Students should have knowledge of linear functions (see Lessons 4.1 through 4.3).

This lesson reinforces the underlying equivalence of a statement, graph, table, and equation for a decreasing linear function.

Teaching the Lesson

Once again, only the statement is given. The teacher can ask, what in the statement indicates the corresponding graph will be linear? (The constant rate of change.) How will this be seen in the table? The change in y will be the same from one entry to the next. What indicates whether the function is increasing or decreasing? (The fact he is walking toward the gate means the distance to the gate is decreasing.)

Homework and Assessment

For homework after finishing the recording sheet, ask students to solve this problem:

> How long did it take Carl to reach the gate? What point on the graph corresponds to this time and distance? Provide the coordinates.

STUDENT RECORDING SHEET

1.

Statement: Carl was 42 feet from the gate and started walking
toward it at rate of 3 feet per second.

Table

Graph

Time	Distance
0	42
1	39
2	36
3	33

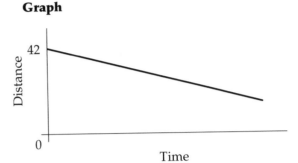

Equation: $y = 42 - 3x$

2. Whole units of time in seconds have been chosen for the table. The units of measurement along the x-axis are seconds. The units of measurement along the y-axis are feet.

3. Answers will vary. Here is an example sentence: After two seconds, Carl was thirty-six feet from the gate.

4. The y-intercept represents Carl's initial distance from the gate. The x-intercept represents the time it took Carl to reach the gate.

HOMEWORK

It took Carl fourteen seconds to reach the gate. This corresponds to the point (14,0).

Extend the Learning: Suppose Carl starts twice as far from the gate. Will it take him twice as long to reach it?
Answer: Yes, it will take Carl twenty-eight seconds to walk eighty-four feet.

Student _____ Class _____ Date _____

Carl at the Gate
Student Recording Sheet

1. Given the statement below, create a table, graph, and equation that represent Carl's distance from the gate in terms of time. (Be sure to label the axes of the graph and the columns of the table.)

> **Statement:** Carl was forty-two feet from the gate and started walking toward it at rate of three feet per second.

Table

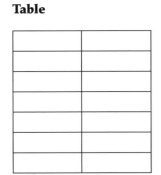

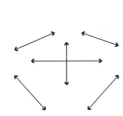

Graph

Equation: _____

2. What are the units of measurement along the *x*-axis? What are the units of measurement along the *y*-axis?

3. Choose a row in the table, and write a statement about the application based on the information provided in that row.

4. What information is provided by the *y*-intercept? What information is provided by the *x*-intercept?

A Rocket in the Air

Work from equation, to description, to graph, to table for a quadratic function.

Overview

Class Time: 20 minutes

Prerequisites: Students should have completed Lessons 2.11, 2.12, 3.7, and 3.8.

This lesson looks at a quadratic function that models a rocket in the air.

Teaching the Lesson

Quadratic functions are studied in algebra and often used to illustrate concepts in calculus. Applications occur in physics and economics. Revenue functions can be modeled by quadratic equations, if the demand and price functions are linear. The standard question "Given x, what is y?" can be answered using substitution. However, answering the question "Given y, what is x?" without a graphics calculator often requires use of the quadratic formula. Using the graph on a calculator, it is possible to estimate the answer or even intersect the horizontal line corresponding to the y-value with the quadratic function using the calculator's "Intersect" feature.

 When using a calculator with a quadratic function, students often have trouble knowing how to set the window. To complete this lesson, students should use the tick marks indicating units along the axes to help set the window.

 Perhaps do this lesson with the whole class and have students do another lesson on their own. (Lesson 4.9 is also a rocket problem.)

 Students will need graphics calculators to complete this lesson.

 MATH MATTERS

A quadratic function is a function of the form $y = ax^2 + bx + c$ where a, b, and c are constants and $a \neq 0$.

Homework and Assessment

For homework after finishing the recording sheet, ask students to solve these problems:

1. If 2 is added to the equation, how will the y-intercept change?
2. What does the change in y-intercept mean in terms of the application?
3. How does the change in y-intercept change the maximum height the rocket will reach?
4. Suppose the x-intercept is 2 greater. What does this mean in terms of the application?

STUDENT RECORDING SHEET

1.

Statement: A rocket was fired from a ten-foot platform
with an initial velocity of eighty feet per second.

Table

Time	Distance
0	10
1	74
2	106
3	106
4	74
5	10

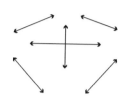

Graph

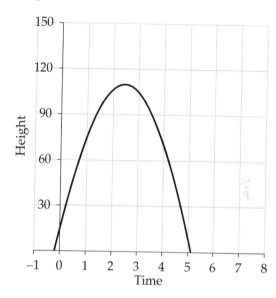

Equation: $y = -16x^2 + 80x + 10$

2. We have chosen to record time for each second. The units of measurement along the x-axis are seconds. The units of measurement along the y-axis are feet.

3. Answers will vary. Here is an example sentence: After four seconds, the rocket was seventy-four feet in the air.

4. The x-intercept is 5.1, and it represents the time the rocket hit the ground (which is also the length of time the rocket was in the air). The y-intercept is ten, and it represents the height above the ground from which the rocket was shot off.

HOMEWORK

1. If 2 is added to the equation, the y-intercept will be two units greater.
2. The change in y-intercept means the rocket was shot off from a platform two feet higher above the ground.
3. The rocket's maximum height is also two feet higher.
4. The change in x-intercept means the rocket hit the ground two seconds later and so was in the air for two seconds longer.

Extend the Learning:

If students have access to and some knowledge of using TI graphics calculators, they can do the following problem, which is similar to Lesson 4.8 and designed to help students set the window for a quadratic function.

When an object is shot into the air with an initial velocity of v_0 feet per second from a height of h_0 feet above the ground, the height of the object (y) in terms of the time since firing (x) can be modeled using this equation:

$$y = -16x^2 + v_0 x + h_0$$

1. Suppose a rocket is fired from a platform eight feet above the ground with an initial velocity of seventy feet per second.
    a. What equation do you put under the $y = $?
    b. If you press "Zoom 6" to graph this equation, what do you see? Does it tell you anything about the rocket?
    c. Is it helpful to zoom out? Is it helpful to zoom in?
    d. Try looking at your table. Where should you start, and what do you want your table shift to be?
    e. Explain how looking at the table helps you set your window.

Answers:

1.
    a. $y = -16x^2 + 70x + 8$
    b. If you press "Zoom 6" to graph this, you will see a jagged line that looks almost vertical at about $x = 4.5$. It tells you that the rocket comes down after about 4.5 seconds.
    c. No, it is not helpful to zoom out or zoom in.
    d. Using the table is very helpful. Start at 0 and go up by 1. You will see that the rocket is in the air for a little over four seconds and reaches its maximum height between two and three seconds.
    e. You can now set your table shift for a smaller number (say, 0.2) and better see how high the rocket will go in the air. A good range for x is from 0 to 5, as we are not interested in the time before the rocket is shot off or after it has hit the ground. The corresponding y-values range from 0 to less than 90, which is also a good range.

Student _____ Class _____ Date _____

Note: You will need a graphics calculator to do this problem.

When an object is shot into the air with an initial velocity of v_0 feet per second from a height of h_0 feet above the ground, the height of the object (y) in terms of the time since firing (x) can be modeled using this equation:

$$y = -16x^2 + v_0 x + h_0$$

1. Suppose a rocket was fired from a platform ten feet above the ground with an initial velocity of eighty feet per second. Fill in all the parts of the following diagram. Use the tick marks representing units on the axes of the graph to help you set the window on your calculator.

Statement: _____

Table

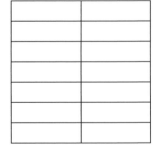

Graph

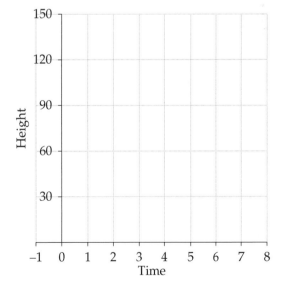

Equation: _____

(continued)

2. Give the units of measurement along the *x*-axis. Give the units of measurement along the *y*-axis.

3. Choose a row in the table, and write a statement about the application based on the information provided in that row.

4. What is the *x*-intercept, and what information does it provide? What is the *y*-intercept, and what information does it provide?

Another Rocket in the Air

Understand quadratic functions.

Overview

Class Time: 20 minutes

Prerequisites: Students should have completed Lessons 2.11, 2.12, 3.7, 3.8, and 4.8.

This lesson looks at a quadratic function that models a rocket in the air.

Teaching the Lesson

In this lesson, students explore the problem of finding x when given y. This is a standard problem for all functions, but it is sometimes difficult for students learning to work with quadratic functions. These students want to proceed algebraically in the same way they did with linear functions.

Students will need graphics calculators to complete this lesson.

Homework and Assessment

For homework after finishing the recording sheet, ask students to solve these problems:

1. Suppose you have been asked to find the time the rocket was 150 feet above the ground using the graph. If you try to use the equation, what equation do you need to solve? What happens when you try to solve for x with this equation?
2. You can also use the table to find out when the rocket was 150 feet in the air. Explain how to do this.
3. On the same set of axes, you can graph the line $y = 150$. What information is provided by the intersection of this line and the original curve? If you have a TI graphics calculator, use the "Intersect" key under the "Calc" menu to find the points of intersection. What do you get when you do this?

STUDENT RECORDING SHEET

1.

Statement: _____

Table

Time	Distance
0	8
1	112
2	184
3	224
4	232
5	208
6	152
7	64

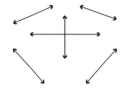

Graph

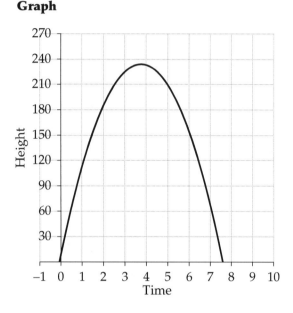

Equation: $y = -16x^2 + 120x + 8$

2. The units of measurement along the x-axis are seconds, and the units of measurement along the y-axis are feet.
3. The rocket was 150 feet in the air after about one and half seconds and again after about six seconds. There are two answers because the rocket reached 150 feet both on its way up and on its way down.
4. The x-intercept is about 7.6, and it represents the time the rocket hit the ground (which is also the length of time the rocket was in the air). The y-intercept is 8, and it represents the height above the ground from which the rocket was fired off.

HOMEWORK

1. You need to solve this equation: $150 = -16x^2 + 120x + 8$. You cannot get x alone in terms of y alone, as both x^2 and x appear in the equation. In more advanced algebra, you will learn the quadratic formula, which is used to solve equations of this type.

1. Suppose you are given the equation $ax^2 + bx + c = 0$, where a, b, and c are constants, $a \neq 0$ and $b^2 - 4ac \geq 0$. The quadratic formula tells you

$$x = \frac{-b - \sqrt{b^2 - 4ac}}{2a} \text{ or}$$

$$x = \frac{-b + \sqrt{b^2 - 4ac}}{2a}$$

2. Go to the table with a table shift of 1, and you will see that y will be at 150 between 1 and 2 and again around 6. Now alter the table shift to 0.5. You will see that the model says the rocket is 152 feet above the ground after 1.5 seconds and again after 6 seconds. Altering your table shift to 0.01 will show the rocket is at 150.55 feet after 1.47 seconds and again after 6.02 seconds.

3. The line and parabola intersect at the times the rocket is 150 feet in the air. The "Intersect" key gives the times 6.0276084 and 1.4723916.

Extend the Learning:

1. When you change h_0 but keep v_0 the same, what condition do you change for the rocket? What choices for h_0 make sense in terms of the application? Choose a new value for h_0, and create a graph, table, and equation using this value. Compare the new graph, table, and equation with the original versions from the lesson recording sheet. How do the graphs compare? How do the tables compare? How do the equations compare?

2. When you change v_0 but keep h_0 the same, what condition do you change for the rocket? What choices make sense for v_0? Choose a new value for v_0, and create a graph, table, and equation using this value. Compare the new graph, table, and equation with the original versions from the lesson recording sheet. How do the graphs compare? How do the tables compare? How do the equations compare?

Answers:

1. You change the height from which the rocket takes off. Any nonnegative number makes sense. Choosing 0 would indicate the rocket is being shot off from the ground. The new graph will be the original graph shifted by $h_0 - 8$ units. This shift will be up if $h_0 - 8$ is a positive number and down if it is a negative number. The new table will likewise shift; for the same x-values, the y-values will shift by $h_0 - 8$ units. In the new equation, the final term will be different and will be your choice of h_0.

2. You change the initial velocity with which the rocket takes off. Any nonnegative number makes sense. An initial velocity of 0 would indicate the rocket is being dropped off from platform. On the new graph, the rocket will go higher and stay in the air longer if your v_0 is larger than 120 and it will not go as high if your choice is less than 120. The new table will also shift. In the equation, the coefficient of the x will be different and will be your choice of v_0.

Student _____ Class _____ Date _____

Another Rocket in the Air

Student Recording Sheet

Note: You will need a graphics calculator to complete these questions.

When an object is shot into the air with an initial velocity of v_0 feet per second from a height of h_0 feet above the ground, the height of the object (y) in terms of the time since firing (x) can be modeled using this equation:

$$y = -16x^2 + v_0 x + h_0$$

1. Suppose a rocket was fired from a platform eight feet above the ground with an initial velocity of 120 feet per second. Fill in all the parts of the following diagram.

Statement: _____

Table

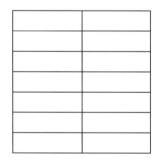

Graph

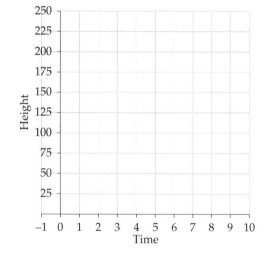

Equation: _____

2. Give the units of measurement along the *x*-axis. Give the units of measurement along the *y*-axis.

3. Use the graph to determine when the rocket was 150 above the ground. Why are there two answers?

4. What is the *x*-intercept, and what information does it provide? What is the *y*-intercept, and what information does it provide?

Index

Algebra, concepts in, 169
Algebraic functions, 114. *See also* Equations
Algebraic knowledge, and graphs/graphing, 2
Answers, correctness of, 9
Axes
   purpose of, 4, 8
   and relationships/functions, 4
   scales of, 54, 60, 90
   variables for, 150
Calculus, concepts in, 14, 124, 169
College students, understanding of graphs/graphing by, 108
Common Core State Standards, 2
Comparing/Contrasting, of multiple curves/graphs, 33, 37
Concavity, of curves/graphs, 14, 81, 90
Constant functions, 114, 157
Continuous vs. discrete data, 114, 117. *See also* Tables, vs. graphs
Correctness, of answers in math, 9
Cost functions, 163
Curves/Graphs
   comparing/contrasting of, 33, 37
   descriptions of. *See* Descriptions
   "lines" as, 37
   and rates of change, 14
   types of, 14, 16, 42, 110. *See also specific types*

Decreasing functions, 19, 27, 30, 65, 85, 95, 153, 166. *See also* Functions, increasing vs. decreasing
Decreasing rates of change, 14, 19, 68, 85, 120. *See also* Rates of change, increasing vs. decreasing
Dependent variables, 14, 71. *See also* Variables
Derivatives, 14
Descriptions, of functions, 2, 45, 48, 50, 54
Discrete vs. continuous data, 114, 117. *See also* Tables, vs. graphs
Distance-vs.-time curves/graphs, 42, 85, 90

Elementary school, math curriculum for, 108
Equations
   for constant functions, 157
   for cost functions, 163
   for linear functions, 144, 146, 150, 153, 160, 166. *See also* Linear functions
   for quadratic functions, 144, 169, 174. *See also* Quadratic functions
Exponential curves, 110

Functions
   algebraic representations of, 2. *See also* Equations
   common difficulties with, 19
   definition of, 4
   descriptions as representations of, 2. *See also* Descriptions
   equations as representations of, 144, 146. *See also* Equations
   graphs as representations of, 2, 54, 110, 153. *See also* Graphs/Graphing
   increasing vs. decreasing, 2, 4, 8, 81. *See also* Decreasing functions; Increasing functions
   multiple representations of, 146, 150, 153, 157, 160
   and rates of change, 14–15. *See also* Rates of change
   tables as representations of, 110, 114, 120, 146. *See also* Tables
   types of, 71, 76, 114, 163, 169. *See also specific types*

Global perspective, for reading graphs, 2, 8, 33
Graphics calculators, use of, 169, 174
Graphs/Graphing. *See also* Curves/Graphs
   and algebraic knowledge, 2
   common difficulties with, 4–5, 153, 157
   history of, 2
   purpose of, 2, 4, 14, 111, 114, 117
   reading of. *See* Reading

Graphs/Graphing (*cont.*)
    as representations of functions, 2, 54, 110, 153.
      See also Functions
    vs. tables, 108, 111, 114, 117. *See also* Tables
Growth (of person), exercises about, 60

Height (of person), exercises about, 60. *See also*
    Projectiles; Rockets
High school students, understanding of
    graphs/graphing by, 4
Horizontal axis. *See x*-axis

Increasing functions, 14–15, 19, 24, 30, 48, 68,
    120, 150, 160. *See also* Functions, increasing
    vs. decreasing
Increasing rates of change, 14, 19, 90, 95. *See also*
    Rates of change, increasing vs. decreasing
Independent variables, 14, 71, 163. *See also*
    Variables
Input/Output values, 114

Linear curves/graphs, 16, 37. *See also* Linear
    functions
Linear functions, 71, 124, 129, 144, 146, 150, 153,
    160, 166. *See also* Linear curves/graphs
"Lines," 37. *See also* Curves/Graphs
Lines of symmetry, definition of, 134
Local perspective, for reading graphs, 33
Logistic curves/graphs, 110

Origin, definition of, 16
Output/Input values, 114

Parabola, definition of, 100
Playfair, William, 2
Points
    common difficulties with, 4–5
    and unit lengths of axes, 56
Points of inflection, definition of, 81, 110
Projectiles, exercises about, 133, 137. *See also*
    Rockets

Quadrants, of *xy* plane, 5. *See also xy* plane
Quadratic functions, 76, 100, 133, 137, 144, 169,
    174

Rates of change
    constant, 124. *See also* Linear functions
    curves/graphs as representations of, 14
    and functions, 14–15, 81, 120, 121
    increasing vs. decreasing, 2, 14, 19, 81. *See also*
      Decreasing rates of change; Increasing rates
      of change
    specified, 24, 27, 30
    tables as representations of, 120, 121
    varying, 24, 27, 30, 42, 48, 50
Reading, of graphs
    common difficulties in, 4–5, 14
    elements in/nature of, 4, 65, 120
    global vs. local perspectives for, 2, 8, 33
Relationships
    and axes, 4. *See also* Axes
    as functions, 4. *See also* Functions
    graphs as representations of, 2
    multiple representations of, 33
Revenue functions, 169
Riemann sum, definition of, 133
Rockets, exercises about, 100, 103, 107, 144, 169,
    174. *See also* Projectiles

Scales, of axes, 54, 60, 90. *See also* Unit lengths
Science teachers, concerns of, 11, 14
Squares, exercises about, 71, 76
Symmetry, lines of, 134

Tables
    vs. graphs, 108, 111, 114, 117
    purpose of, 111, 114, 117
    as representations of functions, 110, 114, 120,
      146. *See also* Functions
    as representations of rates of change, 120, 121.
      See also Rates of change
Time, exercises about, 4, 163

Unit lengths, along axes, 56. *See also* Scales
Units of measurement
    teaching about, 11, 14
    use with graphics calculators, 169

Value, exercises about, 4
Variables
    for axes, 150
    common difficulties with, 2, 144

dependent vs. independent, 14. *See also* Dependent variables; Independent variables
purpose of, 2, 144
Vertical axis. *See y*-axis

x-axis
labeling of, 4, 61
unit lengths of, 56

xy plane
axes of, 4, 8. *See also* Axes
origin of, 16
quadrants of, 5

y-axis
labeling of, 4, 61
unit lengths of, 56
y-intercept, definition of, 60